the many faces of Jack the Ripper

M. J. Trow

PHOTOGRAPHY BY TIM CRADDOCK

SUMMERSDALE

Summersdale Publishers Ltd
46 West Street
Chichester
West Sussex
PO19 1RP UK

Hardback edition: ISBN 1 84024 016 4
Paperback edition: ISBN 1 84024 079 2

Printed and bound in Great Britain.

Acknowledgements

The Many Faces of Jack the Ripper would not have been possible without the support and co-operation of many other faces!

I would first like to pay tribute to five writers who, in the frenetic world of Ripperology, stand out as first class researchers in search of the truth: Donald Rumbelow, whose *The Complete Jack the Ripper* first fascinated me in the subject; Philip Sugden, whose *The Complete History of Jack the Ripper* must be the last word in historical detail; and Paul Begg, Martin Fido and Keith Skinner, who have not only been helpful personally, but whose *Jack the Ripper A-Z* is rightly the Bible of Ripperology.

For the contemporary photographs, my thanks to: Robin Gillis of the Metropolitan Police Museum; Edward Tilley of the Public Record Office; Stewart Evans (I may not agree with his views on Dr Tumblety, but I admire his research enormously); Jonathan Evans of the Royal London Hospital; John Kirkham of Barnardo's; Michael Carter of Getty Images.

To any photograph copyright owner who we have failed to trace, despite exhaustive enquiries, please accept our apologies. We will be pleased to rectify the discrepancy in any future editions.

My thanks to Tim Craddock, a brilliant young photographer with a great future, whose talent helped to unlock the secrets that still lie in the Abyss; and to Paulina, our Mrs Paumier and our corpse in Mitre Square.

To Stewart Ferris and his team at Summersdale, can I say thanks for their enthusiasm and co-operation and to Andrew Lownie, my agent, as always, for his unflagging support of my projects.

Finally, I would like to say the biggest thank you to Carol, my wife, who patiently types out drafts of manuscripts, writes letters, handles faxes and phone calls and is always there.

Contents

Introduction

No; the identity of the diabolical individual has yet to be established, notwithstanding the people who have produced these rumours . . .

Frederick George Abberline,
ex Chief Inspector, Scotland Yard, 1903

RIPPERMANIA

All the films get it wrong. Shortly before the crimson credits, a brightly-painted and very attractive floozy, no more than twenty-five (and usually Barbara Windsor) struts her stuff down a gas-lit studio street, flicking her feather boa from side to side and parading her wares through clouds of dry ice. She smiles at the camera (her client). She says something cockney, like ''Ello, ducks!' and then the shadow crosses her face. It's a shadow we've all seen before, countless times, the top hat and cape of melodrama, the quintessential bogey man. She screams, but it is too late. The knife flashes up, perfectly in time to the screeching violins of the studio orchestra. The knife comes down, again and again, and the blood splashes on the title.

Almost everything about these films is incorrect. All the Ripper's victims were shabbily dressed, from top to toe. There was nothing provocative about them. Four of them were in their forties and looked considerably older. The nights on which they died were all clear. We know from the Almanac for 1888 that the notorious peasouper fogs for which London became famous and which would have aided Jack's getaway, were never a feature of the murders. Although we'd love to believe that Jack was a 'swell', a 'toff', born with a silver spoon in his mouth, the eyewitness accounts we have of him do not mention a cape or a top hat. And we know from medical evidence that at no time did the Ripper stab downwards. His cuts were horizontal and vertical, but upwards, from below.

To the French he is Jacques L'Eventreur; to the Spaniards Jack el Destripador; to the Welsh Jacripa; to the Czechs Jack Rozparovac. What is the universal appeal of this sordid individual whose sole claim to fame is that he murdered and mutilated five defenceless women in the East End of London in the autumn of 1888?

First, there is the horror of his crimes. Jack is now universally recognized as the world's first serial killer. Even in violence-hardened Whitechapel and Spitalfields, the number, viciousness and concentration of the murders appalled society; from the Queen, who insisted the streets be better lit and the detective force improved, to an anonymous East End woman who told a reporter that 'we don't all want ter be murdered!'

A superb knowledge of the area, a familiarity with police beats and a lot of luck led to Jack escaping scot free. That fact alone has led to the legend of Jack the phantom, Jack the ghost, Jack the Invisible Man. And it has led, no less fancifully, to accusations of cover-ups reaching Kennedyne proportions.

I have tried in this book to ignore the ridiculous. Robert Lees, the medium and radical friend of the Labour MP James Kier

Hardie gets no mention other than here because the only verifiable evidence is that his offer to help the police with their enquiries was turned down three times. In his diary for October 2 1888 he wrote: 'offered services to police to follow up East End murders - called a fool and a lunatic!' There were a lot of such men in London in 1888! Neither have I pursued the pointless enquiry into 'Jill the Ripper'. The murder of women by strangulation and their mutilation with a knife is not a woman's M.O. Most women kill with poison or a gun - murder at a distance. The 'hands-on' killing, with its blood and mess, is not the sort of crime that women commit. (Lizzie Borden may have been an exception, hacking her parents to death with an axe in Fall River, 1892, but then Lizzie Borden was acquitted!) Serial murder in fact is not a 'female thing' either. To say there aren't any female serial killers is perhaps untrue in the light of the recent case of Aileen Wuornos in America, but it may be that even she doesn't fulfil the accepted criteria of what a serial killer is.

The real reason for our fascination with Jack is that he wasn't caught. We are creatures of curiosity. It kills us, sometimes, but we keep asking the same questions - Who? Why? Where? What? When? The greatest of these is the first. And we'll keep digging until we find an answer.

Because until we do, Jack is still out there, on those mean streets of what Jack London called the Abyss.

Watching.

Waiting.

And one day, he'll be back.

THE ABYSS

PUNCH, OR THE LONDON CHARIVARI.—September 29, 1888.

THE NEMESIS OF NEGLECT

"THERE FLOATS A PHANTOM ON THE SLUM'S FOUL AIR,
SHAPING TO EYES WHICH HAVE THE GIFT OF SEEING,
INTO THE SPECTRE OF THAT LOATHLY LAIR.
FACE IT—FOR VAIN IS FLEEING!
RED-HANDED, RUTHLESS, FURTIVE, UNERECT,
'TIS MURDEROUS CRIME—THE NEMESIS OF NEGLECT!"

'Red-handed crime - the Nemesis of Neglect' as Punch saw it on September 29 1888. The Ripper's escapes seemed so magical that it was easy to believe he was 'a phantom on the slum's foul air.'

Where hags called women, ghouls in the guise of men,

Live on death-dealing, feed a loathly life,

On the chance profits of the furtive knife.

. . . Whither comes

The haggard hag of the pavement, she,

The victim's victim, whose delirious glee,

Makes mirth a cackling horror; hither shrink

The waifs of passion and the wrecks of drink . . .

. . . Look at these walls; they reek with dirt and damp,

But in their shadows crouched the homeless tramp

May huddle undisturbed the black night through.

Those narrow winding courts - in thought - pursue.

No light there breaks upon the bludgeoned wife,

No flash of day arrests the lifted knife,

There shrieks arouse not, nor do groans affright.

These are but normal noises of the night . . .

. . . Must it be

That the black slum shall furnish sanctuary

To all light-shunning creatures of the slime,

Vermin of vice, carnivora of crime?

Blind Man's Buff - *Punch* September 22 1888

John Griffith London was called Jack too. For seven weeks in the summer of 1902 he lived with the inhabitants of Spitalfields, Whitechapel and Wapping, on his way to a Boer War journalistic assignment that never happened, and to a kind of immortality that ended with an overdose of morphine on November 22 1916.

Those seven weeks are recorded in *The People of the Abyss,* and they changed his life for ever. 'No other book of mine,' he wrote, 'took so much of my young heart and tears as that study of the economic degradation of the poor.' His friend Upton Sinclair remembered that 'for years afterwards the memories of this stunted and depraved population haunted him beyond all peace.'

This kind of social survey was not new. Between 1851 and 1862, Henry Mayhew produced his monumental *London Labour and the London Poor* with its Dickensian freaks and appaling rookeries of Seven Dials and St Giles. But Mayhew, although a rebel, was a figure of the establishment, a product of Westminster School and a co-editor of Punch. Jack London had been born in poverty and understood his subjects all the better because he knew what they were going through - 'the Abyss is literally a huge, man-killing machine...' Similarly, George Sims, secretly delighted to have been taken for the Whitechapel murderer by a coffee-stall proprietor in the area, wrote *How the Poor Live and Horrible London* a year after the murders took place (1889). Charles Booth pioneered the modern social survey with his *Life and Labour of the People* in London (1889 and 1891). Again, Sims and Booth were men of wealth and education. Sims was educated at expensive European universities, wrote as 'Dagonet' and translated Balzac; Booth owned a steamship company and a whole leather industry in Liverpool with his brother Alfred. Only London understood the London of the poor - 'Mr London alone', the *Independent* wrote in 1902, 'has made it real and present to us.'

George R. Sims, the journalist who ventured into the Ghetto and was mistaken for the Whitechapel murderer.

Let me take you down. Catch the Underground to Aldgate East, where legend has it a bellowing cockney voice used to call 'Aldgate East, Aw get aht', and turn left at street level, then left again. You are now on foot, as Polly Nichols was that night in the Autumn of Terror, with Annie Chapman, Liz Stride, Kate Eddowes and Mary Kelly in the weeks that followed.

Across the road is the first of the sights, the first memory of that autumn. It's called The City Darts now and is a Thorley Tavern, but its ornate top storey windows, refurbished in the 1980s, would have looked down on bustling Commercial Street, with its trams and haywagons, the great artery of the East End that led south to the Ratcliffe Highway and the greatest docks in the world. John Pizer, known as 'Leather Apron', drank here, along with his dosshouse mate and only friend in the world, 'Mickeldy Joe'. And it was here, on the raw night of 11 February 1891, that the dangerous and drunken sailor Thomas Sadler picked up the prostitute Frances Coles, also known as Francis Hawkins, Frances Coleman and 'Carrotty Nell'. The buxom girl was found lying in her own blood under the railway arches in Swallow Gardens two days later.

At the best [wrote London] city life is an unnatural life for the human; but the city life of London is so utterly unnatural that the average workman or workwoman cannot stand it . . . [they] are well on their way to the shambles at the bottom of the Abyss.

But Commercial Street is not at the bottom of the Abyss. We have a long way to go. On the wall of The City Darts (in 1888, The Princess Alice) is a plaque telling us that 27 feet to the north lies

The five maps of the murder sites can be found at the back of the book.

The 'City Darts' was 'The Princess Alice' in 1888. It was the haunt of John Pizer - 'Leather Apron'.

the boundary of St Mary, Whitechapel, and the names of proud churchwardens and overseers of the poor are still there, long dead, long forgotten.

On a Saturday, when I followed in the footsteps of the Ripper, the Abyss is a ghost town. The skeletons of Sunday stalls stand deserted on Wentworth and Middlesex Streets. Here and there are narrow, dark memories of London's Abyss - Rose Court and Arun's Place - where weeds grow from the upper ledges and rubbish piles in untended corners. The closed shops, bright with the golds and silvers of Asian fabrics, are still a reminder of the Jewish tailors of the Rag Fair and the earlier, more affluent Huguenot weavers who lived here.

George Sims wrote of the Wentworth Street Rag Fair:

> Here you can obtain anything and everything in the clothing line, from an odd second or third hand boot to a fourth or fifth hand fur-trimmed overcoat.

Wentworth Street today is better known as the street market of Petticoat Lane.

And a handful of years after the Ripper murders, journalist Edwin Pugh wrote:

> This is Wentworth Street - a street of ugly, featureless houses . . . Each ground floor is a shop and the kerb on either side of the road is cumbered with stalls . . . Your companions are mostly women, Jewesses, the majority wearing the black wigs of the matron over their own scanty locks. There are blowsy and haggard mothers of clinging families; and full-blooded girls with dark eyes, languorously bold, ripe red lips and ebon tresses. The men are of two kinds, the frowsy and the flash. Fish and poultry are the articles of commerce in which trade is most brisk . . .

Off Commercial Street to the East lies Old Montague Street, running more or less parallel with Whitechapel Road on its twisting way to Mile End, the Jews' Burial Ground and Tower Hamlets. To your right is Gunthorpe Street, with its green and gold bollards and litter bins with the legend 'Bethnal Green City Challenge' written on them. The street is still cobbled, for all its double yellow lines, and the huge, just-Victorian Commercial Street school still stands here, A.D. 1901. Gunthorpe Street narrows to an archway, which Ripperologist Paul Harrison says was called 'Shit Alley'. It's broader than most and to its right stands Clutterbuck's Alehouse on the Commercial Road. As we emerge into the sunlight, we see the gilded star and crescent of the Great Mosque to remind us that a new prophet has come to the Abyss. A plaque in the archway describes the history of the area, the tall Huguenot houses with their Flemish influence and their large windows that once gave light for the Jacquard looms; and the fact that Petticoat Lane (Middlesex Street) took its name not from Victorian ladies' underwear, but the short overcoats worn by men and made there in Elizabeth the First's time. 'Bloom's Famous Food Products' still marks the boarded up building dated 1886.

It is this building that looked out over George Yard buildings, now demolished, where prostitute Martha Tabram was found dying on a first floor landing of multiple stab wounds in the early hours of 7 August 1888, the day after a Bank Holiday. Many books on the Ripper count plump, plain Martha as the first of Jack's victims. But we must move on . . .

On the left, off Whitechapel Road, which the Victorian writer J.H. Mackay called 'the greatest public pleasure-ground in the East End', and opposite the London Hospital where Thomas Barnardo was a medical student, lies Vallance Road. Then it was called Baker's Row and off that lies Durward Street. It is a desolate place now, the weak November sunshine glancing off the sheets of corrugated iron and black plastic bags piled against them. All that is left of the Ripper's time is a rusting iron bollard, already seventy years old when the killer struck. Where Brady Street joins Durward Street the road narrows. Here, until ten years ago, stood the derelict Board School where Polly Nichols walked with her client on the night of 30-31 August 1888. Beyond that, in what was Buck's Row, lay a

Corrugated iron marks the entrance to Essex Wharf, Buck's Row.

This rusting bollard stands across the road from the pavement where Polly Nichols died.

row of terraced houses, new in the Autumn of Terror, and a series of warehouses known as Essex Wharf. The space of modern Durward Street gives no hint of its dinginess then, and even the ornate manager's house, with its fancy brickwork and tracery, has gone. In the 1920s a garage was built where Polly Nichols lay, her throat gashed, her breath stopped. And the manager's house had become the premises of Rosenberger Coates and Company, 'Makers of Mens' Ties'. Now the faded diagonal markings allow cars to park there, on the pavement where she died. And trees grow there again . . .

Turn back, back into the Abyss, along Chicksand and Heneage Street. Nothing is left there of the Ripper's time. All their buildings are modern. And we are now in Brick Lane, bustling with Balti houses and Bangladeshi video shops. The dazzling colours of the fabrics shine from every window, crowding out the occasional drab shop front of the older Jewish community, still forlornly selling string, twine, cord and paper bags. In the shadow of the subcontinent's emigrants lies a little, forgotten outpost of H Division, Metropolitan Police. 'Help us', posters implore, 'to rid the street of rats' - and two unsolved murders are plastered over its tatty frontage. 'A murder', wrote the social pioneering journalist Elizabeth Harkness, 'gives [East-Enders] two sensations . . . Was the person poisoned or was his throat cut? Did the corpse turn black or did it keep 'till the nails were put in the coffin?'

Right: The last remnant of the Jewish community in the Ghetto.

Far right: A tiny outpost of law and order in the Abyss - the police station in Brick Lane.

On the corner of Brick Lane and Thrawl Street stands the Sheraz Balti House and Hotel. Look up to the very top of the building. The crumbling red stone reminds us that this was The Frying Pan, where Polly Nichols took her last drink at 12.30 a.m. on that fatal Friday. Where she was for the next fifty minutes, we do not know, but at 1.20 a.m. she was just yards away, at 18 Thrawl Street.

The dosshouses have gone now and the modern scene could not be further removed from our image of the Abyss. Yet here, we are in the heart of Jack London's nightmare.

> The colour of life is grey and drab. Everything is helpless, hopeless, unrelieved and dirty. Bath tubs are a thing totally unknown, as mythical as the ambrosia of the gods. The people themselves are dirty, while any attempt at cleanliness becomes howling farce, when it is not pitiful and tragic. Strange, vagrant odours come drifting along the greasy wind and the rain, when it falls, is more like grease than water from heaven. The very cobblestones are scummed with grease.

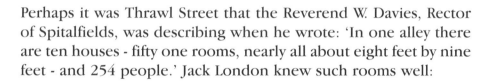

The crumbling sign of 'The Frying Pan', from where Polly Nichols went to her death.

Perhaps it was Thrawl Street that the Reverend W. Davies, Rector of Spitalfields, was describing when he wrote: 'In one alley there are ten houses - fifty one rooms, nearly all about eight feet by nine feet - and 254 people.' Jack London knew such rooms well:

> The little private dosshouses, as a rule, are unmitigated horrors. I have slept in them and I know . . . From the kitchen came the sounds of more genial life . . . But the smell . . . was stronger and a rising nausea drove me into the street for fresh air.

The old rooftops of the dosshouses can still be made out on the walls of Thrawl Street.

The women and children of the Abyss outside the 'White House', the dosshouse at 56 'Flowery Dean'.

If we follow Polly Nichols' faltering footsteps as she roamed the streets, drunk, in search of a client to earn her the 4d she needed for her bed, we are in a pedestrian precinct where neatly dressed Bangladeshi mothers and their children walk quickly to and from the shops. Incongruous wooden palings fence in the Clement Attlee Adventure Playground for the kids. And one of them called to me as I wandered the Abyss, notepad in hand, 'What number are you looking for?' '1888,' I told him and he didn't ask again. J.H. Mackay also experienced the role of the outsider: 'shy, curious eyes followed half in fear, half in hate, the wholly unusual sight of the strangers.'

Only the shadow of the dosshouses remains now. Where men and women jostled in the wooden box beds or huddled by the kitchen fires are now neat, new homes built by the Toynbee Housing Association across which the smells of curry waft.

The journalist T.W. Wilkinson wrote of 'Dosser-land' in 1903:

> For a typical lodging house for men we cannot do better than go to the district of which Spitalfields Church is the centre. Dorset Street, with its squalid air, its groups of 'dossers' scattered over the pavement, as well as Flower and Dean Street . . . are almost under the shadow of that edifice.

'No Ball Games' are to be played in Flower and Dean Walk, a square which, a plaque proudly tells us, was opened by the Prince of Wales on July 18, 1984, and an older memorial, much restored and probably resited, reads 'Erected by the Four Per Cent Industrial Dwellings Company Limited 1886'. The old street line of 'Flowery Dean', one of the most notorious and misnamed streets in London has gone now, vanished forever under the new civics of the end of our century. Polly Nichols, Liz Stride and Kate Eddowes all dossed here in the autumn of 1888. It was still green fields when John Flower and Gowen Dean bought the area in 1655 and even at the height of its notoriety, Nathan Rothschild, head of the richest Anglo-Jewish family in the country, had built the Charlotte de Rothschild Dwellings at one end. Jack London was not impressed.

Flower and Dean Walk as it is today, a far cry from the most squalid street in London in the Ripper's day.

> I stood yesterday in a room in one of the 'Municipal Dwellings' not far from Leman Street. If I looked into a dreary future and saw that if I would have to live in such a room until I died, I should immediately go down, plump into the Thames and cut the tenancy short.

In the year that London shambled across Flowery Dean's greasy cobbles, another rebel walked there - Vladimir Illych Ulyanov, who later called himself Lenin. And six years later, with an altogether lighter step, Abe Saperstein, the founder of the Harlem Globetrotters, was born there.

Beyond the Walk is the Dellow Centre of Providence Row, a brand new building for the destitute of the city, complete with alarms and security cameras - all a far cry from its original counterpart, westward in Crispin Street.

Move north, out of the Walk, out of the square, into Fashion Street. Here, opposite the busy workshops and the clothiers' warehouses, still stands the bizarre Byzantine facade of the arcade built by Abraham Davis in 1905. The street found a kind of immortality in Zangwill's *The Children of the Ghetto*, written in 1892. The houses at Fashion Street's west end are being demolished, the holes of their fireplaces like empty eyes. Jack London knew those rooms:

The corner of Abraham Davis's Byzantine Arcade in Fashion Street.

> It was not a room . . . It was a den, a lair. Seven feet by eight were its dimensions and the ceiling was so low as not to give the cubic air space required by a British soldier to live in barracks . . . Five dollars would have purchased everything in sight. The floor was bare, while walls and ceilings were literally covered with blood marks and splotches. Each mark represented a violent death - of an insect, for the place swarmed with vermin, a plague with which no person could cope single-handed.

And as I walked there, I heard the worried question again, from an adult this time - 'What number are you looking for?' This time it was my turn not to answer. A handwritten sign in a blackened doorway implored earnestly, 'Please, no fucking in the doorway.' Or, if that request didn't work, 'Please pick up your rubbers.' Plus ça change!

Move north again, to Fournier Street, lost in the mighty shadow of Christ Church. London had walked this way too:

> The shadow of Christ Church falls across Spitalfields Garden and in the shadow of Christ's Church, at three o'clock in the afternoon, I saw a sight I never wish to see again. There are no flowers in this garden . . .

The opulence of the Huguenot weavers is still evident in these houses in Fournier Street.

Nicholas Hawksmoor's Christ Church, heart of the parish of Spitalfields.

The church itself is a pale grey, built by Nicholas Hawksmoor between 1714 and 1729 - a more gracious age. Archaeologists digging in its crypt in 1984 found the graves of the Huguenot weavers who probably paid for the building in the first place. It is a forbidding edifice, its entrances wrapped against the atheism of our age with wire mesh. It has long ago dropped divine service. Only the Crypt Centre light still shines - the offer of soup and salvation that General Booth of the Salvation Army would have applauded. In front of it is a superb Edwardian toilet, buried below the Spitalfields street. Like the church, it is padlocked and dead. Maps of 1888 show that it was already a urinal in the Ripper's time. To the church's left as we stand in Fournier Street (Church Street in the Autumn of Terror) is Spitalfields Gardens - 'Itchy Park'. It is small now, with the uprooted gravestones of the worthy citizens resting along its perimeters. It is full of litter, the home of sad-eyed souls drinking something or other out of bottles hidden in brown paper bags. A solitary social worker stood in the playgroup buildings in the park's centre, painting Desperate Dan as part of a mural. More than anywhere else in the Ripper's London, 'Itchy Park' is the saddest, the most desperate. Stand still here and listen to Jack London's voice above the roar of the traffic - 'The City of Dreadful Monotony . . . The City of Degradation'.

Fournier Street itself attempted to challenge the vast Anglican monument that Hawksmoor left. A Huguenot chapel was built there in 1742, which in time became a Methodist chapel (1809). Reflecting the influx of Russian and Polish Jews later in the century, a synagogue was built here by the Orthodox Machzikei Hadath in 1897. It is now a mosque. Thus have Yahweh and Allah held sway in the heart of the Abyss.

Stand in the shadow of Christ Church and you are on the doorstep of The Ten Bells, briefly re-christened 'The Jack the Ripper'. The pub was decked out in the 1970s in Victorian trappings and the names of Jack's targets were painted on its walls - 'One of these unfortunate victims was last seen leaving these premises.' The pub's upper windows with their fine porticoes are still there, but the place is dark and padlocked, as though the East End is suddenly embarrassed by its most infamous son.

There is some doubt as to who the victim was. It may have been Annie Chapman, drinking there at five in the morning 'near Spitalfields Market', which is across the road. Alternatively, it could have been Mary Kelly, who lived (and died) in Dorset Street, a hundred yards away.

North, to Hanbury Street, at the furthest end of the Ghetto. This was once, in more rural and affluent days, called Brown's Lane

The Ten Bells today, where Polly Nichols and Mary Kelly drank, is dead and deserted.

These houses looked down on the first known example of Jack's handiwork in Hanbury Street.

after its landowner in the late 17th century. It was renamed in 1803 after the Quaker brewer Sampson Hanbury and the brewery now owned by Truman's still stands on the site. The four storey house at Number 29, where Mrs Hardyman sold cats' meat and where Annie Chapman was strangled and butchered on the night of September 8 1888, has gone. The bland, modern wall of the brewery, with its broken frosted windows and pale bricks, gives no clue now of the horror of the place. Only the gaunt chimneys of the row opposite remind us of the narrow, busy thoroughfare whose Mission Hall held the radical working class meetings of the Ripper's day. Annie Besant, the Bryant and May match girls' heroine, spoke there, as did Eleanor, the daughter of Karl Marx. The street boasted eight pubs in the Ripper's day.

'Dark Annie' was the most northerly of the Ripper's victims. We must turn back south.

Elizabeth Stride was killed away from the claustrophobic tangle of streets called by George Sims the Ghetto and by Jack London the Abyss. We have to cross the broad thoroughfare of Commercial Road, that leads east to Limehouse. Today, Berner Street is Henriques Street and a large Edwardian building carries the laced initials SBL and the date 1903. An old door is marked 'Cookery Laundry' and the Bangladeshi Youth Movement building stands opposite the Harry Gosling Infant School. At the Commercial Road end is a derelict patch, like a tooth torn from a gum, the basement of the former house littered with rubbish and the inevitable mattress. The far end has given way to modern flats. Somewhere beyond the tiny cluster of general stores in the street's centre once stood a row of four houses and a spoked wheel on the wall marked the entry to Dutfield's Yard, where coaches were built and sackcloth was woven in the Autumn of Terror. Here stood the International Workingmen's Educational Club, dominated then by Eastern European Jews, a pub and the greengrocer's shop belonging to Matthew Packer, a witness who

Nothing marks the site where Polly Nichols died but the blank wall of this brewery.

The Sir John Cass School dwarfs Mitre Square today.

There were three ways out of Mitre Square. Kate Eddowes used none of them.

'Dosset Street' as Dorset Street was known at the time of the Whitechapel murders. Not even the lines of this street remain today.

The last Ripper site. Somewhere under the carpark on the right is Dorset Street and Miller's Court.

became a nuisance during police enquiries into the Whitechapel murders.

The saddest of the murder sites is Mitre Square, where the disembowelled body of Kate Eddowes was found, lying on the pavement in the early morning of September 30 1888, the second victim (or was she?) of the infamous 'double event'. We have moved west now, along Commercial Road and Whitechapel High Street, and have come to Aldgate and to Houndsditch. To our left runs the Minories where Dr Lionel Druitt is alleged to have had a surgery and from which his cousin, Montague, is said to have crept out on unsuspecting nights to carve his name with pride on the bodies of five unfortunates. Ahead is Leadenhall Street, where the East India Company had its headquarters until that all-powerful organisation was broken up thirty years before Jack. This is Moravian country where a blue plaque attests to the fact that John Wesley felt his heart 'strangely moved' there, at a church service of that sect in 1738, before starting his long and lonely road to salvation.

The traffic roars along Aldgate High Street, but the colossal 1930s Sir John Cass School that flanks the Square cuts out the noise. It is a silent, desolate place. Here lay Orange Market, Kearley and Tonge's tall warehouses and the Great Synagogue. This in turn fell to the Luftwaffe's bombs in 1941 - no doubt a source of much rejoicing in the Aryan airfields of the Reich. There are still three ways into the Square and three ways out, although Kate Eddowes used none of them, not of her own free will at least. Three cottages and a high fence formed a right angle within a stone's throw of the City boundary. It was here that Kate's body was found. Legend has it that the place was haunted long before the Ripper by a murderous monk from the Priory of the Holy Trinity, built there in 1108. Mitre Square is palpably richer than the Abyss. We are here in the glass-fronted, opulent world of the Stags and the Bears. London has once more moved on.

There is one more sight to see. Or rather not to see. For of all the Ripper murder sites, the hardest to conjure up is the dingy death room of 13 Miller's Court, off Dorset Street. In its day, it was known locally as 'Dosset' Street for the almost continuous chain of dosshouses that ran its length. It lies under the new multi-storey car park opposite Christ Church, south of the vast and gloomy Spitalfields Market, built to boost trade in the area from 1889. On a Sunday the Market is thriving, with secondhand clothes stalls, antiques and a vast children's gyroscope. On a Saturday it is cavernous and dead. A painfully thin black cat came out to watch me from the building opposite, like one of those Mrs Hardyman catered for in Hanbury Street.

As I crossed to the White's Row car park, a white police car, all sirens

Artillery Passage where the chestnut seller Mrs Paumier was accosted by Jack.

and flashing lights, hurtled past, faster and more direct than those bobbies of the Autumn of Terror, clattering over the cobbles in their hobnailed boots and blowing their shrill whistles to the night. There are warehouses here still with their rusting pulley wheels jutting against the sky and beyond what was the narrow entrance to Miller's Court lies the Tenter Ground, no longer the wide space where linen was bleached in the sun and 'no man may steal it on pain of death'. The huge Refuge for the Poor, marked as a Catholic Convent on the Ordnance Survey map of 1894, still has its 'Men' and 'Women' carved over the unwelcoming doors on Crispin Street.

Jack London spent time in the Whitechapel workhouse, known as the 'Spike'.

> I have been to the spike and slept in the spike and eaten in the spike; also, I have run away from the spike.

We have already wandered past The Britannia where Mary Kelly drank with her genial hosts, Walter and Matilda Ringer and the Horn of Plenty where Jack's last victim drank with Danny Barnett and Julia Venturney on the night of her death. Crossingham's Lodging House stood here and John McCarthy's chandler's shop.

Ahead lies Artillery Passage, where Mrs Paumier, the chestnut seller, swore she was accosted by Jack the Ripper. It once boasted the finest Georgian shopfronts in London, but it is an eerie place now, and gives us the best idea yet of the claustrophobia of the Abyss and the gloom of the Ghetto.

Henry VIII's artillery ground stood here in 1537 when the scarlet-coated gunners fired their culverins and sakers to the cheers of an awestruck crowd.

In older days, Henry VIII's cannon roared across what were open fields here.

We have circled the Abyss. We have crossed the Ghetto. With its smells of curry and its Asian street names, it is difficult to cross the years. We must let Jack London remind us:

> On the benches on either side Leman Street, we cut off to the left into Spitalfields and dived into Frying-Pan Alley. A spawn of children cluttered the slimy pavement . . . In a narrow doorway, so narrow that perforce we stepped over her, sat a woman with a young babe, nursing at breasts grossly naked and libelling all the sacredness of motherhood.

S. Gelberg knew the Ghetto too, writing of it the year after London went there:

> Kosher restaurants abound in it; kosher butcher shops are clustered in thick bunches in its most hopeless parts (seven of them at the junction of Middlesex Street and Wentworth Street) . . . a game of cricket on the broad spaces of Bell Lane or the green fields of Frying-Pan Alley.

And George Sims was never far behind:

> Right in the full tide of East-End life is the corner of Leman Street. Standing there one can see the ever-changing multitudes that throng through Whitechapel High Street, the Commercial Road East and Commercial Street. Type is writ large in the crowds that eddy round you and the alien Jew is most pronounced of all.

Sims was also struck by the almost total lack of transport:

> After you have passed Aldgate Station the hansom becomes rarer and rarer. A little way beyond Leman Street it is practically extinct.

Let London's be the last word on the Abyss:

> East London is such a ghetto, where the rich and the powerful do not dwell and the traveller cometh not and where two million workers swarm, procreate and die.

. . . AND ITS PEOPLE

So one is forced to conclude that the Abyss is literally a huge man-killing machine and when I pass along the little out-of-the-way streets with the full-bellied artisans at the doors, I am aware of a greater sorrow for them than for the 450,000 lost and hopeless wretches dying at the bottom of the pit . . . Four hundred and fifty thousand is a whole lot of people. I should not like to hear them all talk at once. I wonder if God hears them?

Jack London, *The People of the Abyss,* 1903

The fortunes of a great city ebb and flow and the flotsam of those tides are its people. Whitechapel and Spitalfields had not always been at the heart of London's shame and degredation.

The white chapel itself was either the church of St Mary de Mattefelon, referred to in 1340, or the white chapel by Aldgate, the 'ale gap' which ran out of the medieval city to the north east. To the north lay the fields of the Hospital of St Mary, which was known by 1561 as Spitalfields. In Tudor times, the communities beyond the City Wall were growing fast, incorporating the scattered county hamlets of Ratcliffe, Shoreditch, Whitechapel and Spitalfields. Trades could flourish here because of low rents and because the strangulating grip of the guilds, the City Livery Companies, did not reach beyond the Wall. By the 17th century, the 'East End' had already emerged as the manufacturing area of London, spreading like an octopus in all directions.

It was the 17th century that saw a startling cosmopolitan influx to the area. Flemings, Walloons and Dutchmen, encouraged by the success of 'Dutch William' (William III) who was offered the throne on a parliamentary plate in 1688, brought their silk-weaving skills and settled. For all the moans of the 'indigenous' East Enders about Jewish immigrants at the time of the Ripper murders, the 'original' Jewish community was in fact as old or older than theirs. Oliver Cromwell, an oddly tolerant man and effectively the power in the state in the 1650s, had allowed the immigration of Jews for the first time since their expulsion by Edward I in 1290. The Sephardic Jews, with their Old Sephardi graveyard of 1657, were followed by the Ashkenazi Jews early in the 18th century. Like the Flemings, most of these were clothiers and tailors and the houses that sprang up along the edge of the Artillery Ground rattled and hummed to the music of the looms.

The ethnic group that dominated however was the Huguenots, the French Protestants driven west by Louis XIV's sudden revocation of the Edict of Nantes (1689), which denied all but Catholics the right to worship freely. By 1700 there were five Huguenot churches in the Whitechapel/Spitalfields parishes, with names like L'Hopital, La Patente and Du Marché. Spitalfields and Soho - 'Little France' - were areas of heaviest settlement.

The next wave of immigration came in the 1840s when over 300,000 Irish men, women and children scrambled east in an attempt to save themselves from the slow starvation of the Famine. Three times in 1845-6 the vital potato crop failed, the 'praties' turning black in the ground and squelching under the spade. A million people died. The lucky ones got out. Something of the flavour of the Irish was still there in the Ripper's time. Miller's Court where Mary Kelly lived was known locally as McCarthy's rents. Kelly herself almost certainly had Irish origins and Thomas Conway, the husband of Kate Eddowes, was also known as Thomas Quinn, an ex-private of the 18th Royal Irish Foot.

The Irish readily took to the sweated rag trade, elbow to elbow in narrow, dusty rooms as the more affluent Huguenots moved out and the Jews went north to Bethnal Green. The Irish had a reputation of being 'beyond the pale'. They drank and fought and whored. Those more refined drifted away.

On March 1 1881, Tsar Alexander II, returning from a review of his troops in St Petersburg, had his legs all but blown off by a radical group called The People's Will. His son Alexander III, who succeeded the 'Tsar Liberator' later that day, ordered swift reprisals against known dissidents throughout the Empire. The wrath of the righteous fell most heavily on the Jews of Russia and Poland, whose very existence was coupled in the anti-Semitic world of St Petersburg society with revolution. Pogrom followed pogrom and the Jews fled west, settling in various countries as they went. Arriving at London docks, then the largest in the world, they drifted a few hundred yards north to that tight little cluster of streets under the shadow of Hawksmoor's Christ's Church. They set up their own sweated tailoring shops, usually employing less than ten workers because no laws had yet been devised to control businesses that small. Synagogues replaced chapels, Shabbas became the Holy Day and the people of the Abyss grew restive. One of them said to Jack London: 'But 'ow about this 'ere cheap immigration? The Jews of Whitechapel, say, a-cutting our throats right along?'

Like all ghettoes, the Abyss became a self-contained unit, an outland. By the time of the Ripper murders, the Jewish community had occupied perhaps 80 percent of it and this was to grow to 95 percent by the end of the century. As the West End became gentrified and increasingly respectable, the working class moved east, retreating in the face of the furious advance of high rents and civic greed. Jack London reported that in Whitechapel, two-room houses that recently rented for ten shillings had since

Two symbols of authority in Aldgate that barely touched the Abyss - the church and the law.

In the ghetto, poverty was endemic. This abandoned soup kitchen in Brune Street once saved lives.

more than doubled their rents. Chronic overcrowding resulted. London again:

> In St Georges-in-the-East a man and his wife and their family of eight occupied one small room. This family consisted of five daughters, aged twenty, seventeen, eight, four and an infant; and three sons, aged fifteen, thirteen and twelve. In Whitechapel a man and his wife and their three daughters, aged sixteen, eight and four, and two sons, aged ten and twelve years, occupied a smaller room . . . Not only are the houses let, but they are sub-let and sub-let down to the very rooms.

The teeming Ghetto was home to nearly half a million people in 1888 and, typical of working class areas everywhere in the 19th century, it had two types - the employed and the down and out.

There was a bewildering variety of trades in Whitechapel and Spitalfields. A breakdown of those who gave evidence at the inquests of the Ripper's victims reveals an engraver, a caretaker, a fruiterer, an undertaker, a newspaper editor, a mortuary attendant, a lampblack packer and a match girl. There are street porters, carmen and bootmakers in numbers; tailors, pawnbrokers, bakers and cigar makers; owners of penny gaffs and dockers and horsekeepers. The street directories for 1888 give us the names of others not spotlighted by Jack's 'funny little games'. In Berner Street, where Elizabeth Stride died, Edwin Sumner was a greengrocer, John Simkin was a chemist, Henry Norris ran a general store and the Jewish element was represented by Louis Hagens who ran an off-licence and Louis Friedman who baked unleavened bread. S. Gelberg, visiting Whitechapel in 1903, wrote:

> You are in a city of endless toil. All day long and far into the night the factories make dismal music in the Ghetto . . . 'Weiber! Weiber! Leimische Beigel!' sing out the women . . . and long after the shadows have lengthened . . . they are still vouching by their own lives or the kindness of Shem Yisboroch (God) to Israel for the quality of their wares. So spins the toiling Ghetto round its daily orbit.

In Crispin Street, around the corner from the murder site of Mary Kelly, Isaac Mendoza sold furniture and Myers Markos made tinplate toys. In the same street were beer retailers, farriers, basket makers, saddlers and sack makers, all endlessly toiling to the Ghetto's dismal music. Along Fashion Street, where Abraham

Davis would build his curious Byzantine arcade, rag merchants like Solomon Silver, Moses Rosenthal, Michael Goldstein and Wolff Lessar vied with each other to make the Ghetto their promised land.

These were the people Jack London felt most sorry for - the 'full bellied artisans at the doors'. George Sims felt it too:

> The people to watch if you want to dive beneath the crust of the kerb commerce are the men and women who have no stalls . . . very poor and miserable they look as a rule; their faces are anxious, their voices are weak. You may watch them for hours and not see them take a farthing. But on their takings depends their bed that night . . .

But the group that horrified respectable citizens of the West End were the others, those who 'carried the banner' (wandered the streets) all night. T.W. Wilkinson specialized as a journalist in workhouses.

> 'Where did you sleep last night?' asks the porter. 'Nowhere' . . . The key of the street; dropping asleep on a doorstep or, worse still, while still walking . . . dodging about in the cold, grey dawn to get a wash at a street fountain when a policeman is not looking

What divided those who coped from those who could not, was work. There were still no regulations about wages or a fair day's pay for a fair day's work. Ben Tillett was yet to strike for the 'dockers' tanner' and the army of gas workers had not mobilized. Unskilled men and their women had to fight for every crumb of comfort. Unemployment was not merely unfortunate. It was literally lethal. Jack London describes one example.

> He had fought and starved and suffered [unable to find work] for eighteen months. He got up one September morning early. He opened his pocket knife. He cut the throat of his wife, Hannah, aged thirty-three. He cut the throat of his firstborn, Frank, aged twelve. He cut the throat of his son, Walter, aged eight. He cut the throat of his daughter, Nellie, aged four. He cut the throat of his youngest-born, Ernest, aged sixteen months. Then he watched beside the dead all day until the evening, when the police came . . .

If we trace the footsteps of the curious journalists and do-gooders who entered the Abyss, we are faced with a busy, jostling, appalling scene which has gone for ever. A. St John Adcock remembered a typical Saturday night:

> As we push further east the crowd becomes denser and livelier; an incongruously blended multitude in which abject squalor elbows coquettish elegance and sickly misery and robust good-humour and frank poverty and poverty decently disguised and lean knavery and leaner honesty, drunkenness and sobriety, care and frivolity . . . all hustle or loiter side by side, in one vast, motley, ever-moving panorama.

Graham Hill wrote of London pubs:

> Nearby, in Whitechapel Road, there is to be seen an open bar - the only one of its kind in London - where . . . customers stand on the pavement about the pewter-topped window-ledge and imbibe their refreshments in sight of passers-by . . . In the Clothing Exchange, locally known as the 'Rag Fair' which lies off Middlesex Street, thousands of people assemble on the Sabbath to sell and purchase ready-made and remade clothes.

George Sims took up the tale:

> Down the little dark side streets around Whitechapel and Spitalfields you will find curious little shops that deal principally in olives and gherkins in salt and water. The latter are exposed in big tubs and are often bought and eaten without ceremony on the spot . . . There are even small refreshment counters and little coffee shops in which the menu is entirely in Yiddish . . . The pie shops here offer you a more varied choice than in the west . . . You can buy hot beef-steak pies and puddings, eel, kidney, meat, fruit and mince pies . . . Here, in all its glory the eel-jelly trade is carried on . . . Many a time on a terribly cold night have I watched a shivering, emaciated-looking man eagerly consuming his cup of eel-jelly and only parting with the spoon and crockery when even the tongue of a dog could not have extracted another drop from either . . . Under the flaring naphtha lights are set out scores of little saucers containing whelks, cockles and mussels 'a penny a plate' . . . Hot green peas are served in teacups . . . And in the east you may also purchase

peanuts fresh roasted . . . The hot apple fritter is now, too, a street stall luxury . . . The hot fruit drink is a favourite light refreshment in the East End where a large number of Hebrew immigrants have no taste for the more potent beverages of the gin palace and the tavern.

D.L. Woolmar informed his appalled and fascinated readers that:

> Slum-land . . . thrives on neglect and only asks to be let alone . . . Over no other part of the kingdom . . . do the two angels of life and death hover more continually; and nowhere . . . is the fight between good and evil more fierce and stubborn . . . Thirst is, indeed, the chief complaint of the community . . . In old and respectable houses of the next parish of Spitalfields, which once held weavers and their looms, more foreign Jews and Jewesses, perhaps ten in one room, stir in the beds which they have made up on the floor . . . [they] must be off before the inspector's hour of duty. He has an English prejudice against overcrowding . . .

Wentworth Street as Gustav Doré saw and engraved it in 1872. Already a slum, the street was at the heart of the Jewish Rag Fair.

St. John Adcock compared the East and West Ends of a Sunday evening:

> . . . we have gone up Eastcheap, through the Minories into Aldgate and from Aldgate away down Commercial Road East, past dingy coffee-rooms where Jews and Christians, Britishers and aliens, sit at bare wooden tables in clouds of tobacco smoke, reading, meditating, sipping their drinks or beguiling the time with dominoes . . . past numerous public houses where men and women are sociably regaling themselves; past large and small sweet-stuff and pastry shops, wherein juvenile Don Juans of the district are lolling gloriously at the counters treating themselves and their 'donahs' to ices and ginger-beer . . . and in Commercial Road and Whitechapel Road and the tangle of streets that intersect them, the many shops, mostly Jewish, that are open have lighted up their windows and made those that are shut look deader than ever by contrast . . . Diverging up Osborn Street, Whitechapel . . . we come upon waggons standing by the roadside, some horseless and their shafts up, others already horsed . . . one after another they move rumbling away and vanish in the direction of the docks . . . and in the very small hours of the morning they will be toiling heavy laden into London's markets.

The tenter ground was already a dangerous slum by the Ripper's time.

In all the back streets and alleys hereabouts people are leaning from their windows, sitting on their doorsteps, obstructing the pavements or strolling in the roads, taking the air, with a tendency to gravitate towards corners and stop there. Nearly every corner here and throughout Spitalfields has its knot of cosmopolitan babblers of both sexes . . . As you retrace your steps along Aldgate, look into Middlesex Street . . . which until after noon was a seething, roaring fair through which one had almost to fight a passage . . . [now] the 'lane' is so utterly deserted that the few children playing at leapfrog over its littered stones look lost in it.

From an early hour of the evening one side of Aldgate and one side of Whitechapel Road have been promenaded from end to end by an apparently interminable crowd of boys and girls, youths and maidens, men and women, shabby and repectable, elegant and super-elegant, chattering, laughing, jostling, perambulating . . .

Sims observed the haggling of the patterers:

> In the Whitechapel Road there are kerbstone auctioneers, knockers-down of old clothes and patched up umbrellas, who will patter the whole night . . . 'I ask no more, I take no less.' That is the ultimatum.

William Ryan saw beauty in the gloom:

> On Saturdays particularly, baskets and barrows of flowers make many bright splashes in High Street, Whitechapel . . . The passers-by are mostly Jews . . . Working men returning home buy large bunches of loose flowers in Whitechapel to brighten their humble tenements on Sunday. The weary-looking factory girls cannot resist the temptation to take half a dozen roses for a penny.

Jack London was instinctively drawn, as Lord Shaftesbury had been before him, to the children:

> There is one beautiful sight in the East End and only one and it is the children dancing in the street when the organ-grinder goes his round. It is fascinating to watch them, the new-born, the next generation, swaying and stepping . . . with muscles that move swiftly and easily and bodies that leap airily, weaving rhythms never taught in dancing school . . . But there is a Pied Piper of London Town who steals them away. They disappear.

As Edwin Pugh spoke of the children of the Ghetto:

> Children are begotten in drunkenness, saturated in drink
> before they draw their first breath, born to the smell and
> taste of it and brought up in the midst of it.
>
> A troop of noisy children are playing hopscotch opposite
> the door, from which the weather has worn the paint,
> leaving on its panels as sole embellishment sundry names,
> dates and rhymes - rude memorials to the general
> usefulness of local pocket-knives, nails and hairpins . . . A
> slight push and you are in the passage, noting the dirty
> broken walls, to which cling a few patches of greasy
> wallpaper . . . There is no sunshine to speak of outside . . .
> Women with unkempt hair and unwashed faces pop their
> heads out of half-opened doors and eye the intruder with a
> rather aggressive air. Visitors are not welcome here . . .
>
>   And all the while . . . they [East End girls] have to play
> another part of little mother to younger brothers and sisters.
> They ape, with a cruel fidelity, the methods of stern parents,
> sometimes covering their charges with abuse, slapping,
> shaking, tousling them . . . In short, they are serving their
> apprenticeship to life . . . For though she plays, the poor
> little girl of the London streets is never quite a child.

'Never quite a child. . . 'Edwin Pugh is coy about prostitution, but
it was the way of life for many East End girls. Child prostitution
was a notorious racket in the 19th century, until a journalist, W.T.
Stead, exposed it by buying a girl of thirteen for five pounds and
writing up the story as 'The Maiden Tribute of Modern Babylon'
in the *Pall Mall Gazette*, three years before the Ripper struck.
Children were lured to London by the 'Whittington syndrome' -
the streets were paved with gold and with magic. Girls and boys
often ended up bewildered by the exotic sights, the carriages and
the bands and the penny gaffs. Girls of ten to fourteen were
highly prized by 'gentlemen' out on a spree and their virginity
was lost for the first time, time and time again, thanks to the
ingenuity of the madames who ran the brothels and a little
chicken blood. The beautiful ones, the clever ones, became
courtesans and kept women, living in luxury in rooms in Duke
Street and James Street in the West End. Jack London makes a
veiled reference to them:

> And I wondered where these women were and heard a
> 'harlot's ginny laugh'. Leman Street, Waterloo Road,
> Piccadilly, The Strand, answered me, and I knew where
> they were.

The others, as their charms began to fade, drifted east into the Abyss, where London saw them, on the streets:

> But the girl of fourteen or fifteen, forced in this manner to leave the one room called home . . . can have but one end. And the bitter end of that one end is such as that of the woman whose body the police found this morning in a doorway in Dorset Street, Whitechapel. Homeless, shelterless, sick, with no-one with her in her last hour, she had died in the night of exposure . . . She died as a wild animal dies.

Clients wandering the East End in search of a cheap thrill bumped into 'Unfortunates' or 'Ladies of the Night' (the middle class Victorians were past masters at euphemisms) who conventionally would ask 'Are you good natured, dearie?' If they were, a cash transaction would then take place (the usual fee was 6d or even 4d - the price of a dosshouse box bed) and business would be conducted in the darkness of the labyrinthine courts and alleyways that crisscrossed the Abyss. Of the Ripper's five victims, only one, Mary Kelly, had a rented room to which to take her client - 'Come along. You will be comfortable.' It measured ten feet by six, but it was home - at least until the morning of Lord Mayor's Day, 1888. The others nipped along the shadows of Buck's Row, into a back yard in Hanbury Street, an entranceway in Berner Street or the silent corner of an empty square. Few commentators have realized that intercourse standing up and from behind was believed by most prostitutes to be a means of avoiding pregnancy. It was also a classic pose of defencelessness. One fierce jerk with an arm or hand around the neck followed by the flash of a knife and it is certain that Polly Nichols, Annie Chapman, Liz Stride and Kate Eddowes would never 'carry the banner' again. Mary Kelly was different - but Mary Kelly was different in all sorts of ways. We shall meet them all later.

As disturbing as the existence of about 80,000 prostitutes in the East End as a whole was the vast number of vagrants who haunted the Abyss. Jack London lived among them.

> 'On the doss', they call vagabondage here . . . kipping or dossing . . . is the hardest problem they have to face . . . The inclement weather and the harsh laws are mainly responsible for this, while men ascribe their homelessness to foreign immigration, especially of Polish and Russian Jews, who take their places at lower wages and establish the sweating system.

They begged on the streets, they queued for hours to enter 'the spike', the Whitechapel workhouse or the Providence Row Night refuge. And when all that had failed, they died in the freezing doorways of a desolate night.

Such demoralization was compounded by that other great social evil of the Victorians - drink. There were eight pubs along the short stretch of Hanbury Street, three in Dorset Street (I counted its ghostly length as 640 paces), an estimated eighty on- and off-licences in the right angle formed by Commercial Street and Whitechapel Road. William Nichols left his wife Polly because of her drinking; Annie Chapman was described as 'drunken and immoral'; 'Long Liz' Stride was arrested eight times in the year before her death for drunkenness; Annie Eddowes told an inquest that her mother's marriage had collapsed because of Kate's heavy drinking; and Mary Kelly was heard singing drunkenly only hours before she died.

If the women turned to drink as a refuge, so did the men and they added violence, too. Jack London saw the sights:

> To pound one's wife to a jelly and break a few of her ribs is a trivial offence compared with sleeping out under the naked stars because one has not the price of a doss.
>
> They become indecent and bestial. When they kill, they kill with their hands . . . They gouge a mate with a dull knife . . . They wear remarkable boots of brass and iron and when they have polished off the mother of their children with a black eye . . . they knock her down and proceed to trample her . . .

What was the solution to the vicious downward spiral, in an age before the Welfare State, organized Trade Unions and the Labour Party? Most turned a blind eye. They believed, and their fathers had said it openly, that poverty was crime self-inflicted by the poor. Self-help was the answer. And if that didn't work? Well, they were harlots, and vagabonds and Jews, so what did it matter?

It did matter to a few and before Charles Booth's surveys and the horrified wanderings of Jack London and George Sims, some of them were there, shoulder to shoulder in the Abyss, making a noise, causing a stir.

One was Thomas Barnardo, the Irishman who trained at the London Hospital and who talked to Liz Stride on the night she died. In the year of the Ripper, he wrote his *Three Tracts*:

> In cellar, in garret, in alley and court,
> They weep and they suffer and pine,
> And the wolves of the city are prowling near.
> Back, wolves. For the children are mine.

'Back, wolves: for the children are mine' - Dr Thomas Barnardo saved the lives of thousands of children of the Abyss in his own lifetime and his organisation has gone on doing so ever since.

Ragged street urchins like this one lived - and died - in the teeming misery of the Abyss.

There are those who have accused Barnardo of fabricating his evidence, of 'scruffing up' perfectly well-nourished children to exaggerate his tales of poverty and neglect. But then, there are those who accuse him of being Jack the Ripper! When he founded a ragged school and shelter in Stepney, a mudlark called Jim Jarvis took him on a tour of Aldgate and Houndsditch:

> It seemed as though God himself had suddenly pulled aside the curtain which concealed from my view the untold miseries of child life upon the streets of London.

The heartbreak never left him. In 1870, he set up a home for twenty-five destitute boys at Stepney Causeway. The twenty-sixth, eleven year old John Somers, known as 'Carrots', whom Barnardo had turned away, was found dead from exposure in an alley in Billingsgate. Barnardo put up a sign and meant it - 'No destitute child ever refused admission.'

Barnardo carried the banner with the dossers. He knew the courts and alleyways as well as they did, but with funds from Lord Shaftesbury was able to bring some comfort to the Abyss. He bought the lodging house at Number 32, 'Flowery Dean' and turned it into a shelter for boys at 1d a night. A hot meal cost ½d but no one was turned away and no one went hungry. One of the women who supported his cause was 'Long Liz' herself, so soon to become the Ripper's victim. The police brought down and outs to Number 32 and terrified women hammered on Barnardo's doors in the darkness.

By 1905 Barnardo had built schools, convalescent homes and training centres, 102 buildings in all. Later that year he died of overwork.

The less human face of charity was that of Canon Samuel Barnett, the vicar of St John's, one of the grimmest parishes in London. He and his wife Henrietta were fighters and considerably improved the lot of the poor, but he was of the old school which advocated a vigorous self-help

> I would say the poor starve because of the alms they receive . . . It is a sin which we are here to fight.

The Barnetts gave their comfortable vicarage over as a school for adults as well as children and lived in the slum alley of Crown Court. Four years before the Ripper struck, the Canon was made warden of Toynbee Hall (still there along Commercial Street) where sixteen Oxford graduates trained as what today would be called social workers. He brought culture to the East End - choirs and lectures. Basil Henriques spoke there (and they later named

Samuel Barnett - the Rector of Spitalfields who believed in self-help and muscular Christianity.

Liz Stride's murder street after him); so did the young Clem Atlee. With the Rothschilds, he set up the Four Per Cent Dwellings Company and replaced the labyrinthine warrens of Thrawl Street and Flower and Dean.

Unlike Barnardo, Barnett had a comment to make on the Ripper murders:

> The murders were . . . bound to come; generation could not follow generation in lawless intercourse, children could not be familiarized with scenes of degredation . . . and the end of all be peace.

And in his suggestions as to the remedy, he railed against the social injustice of his day - light the streets because 'dark passages lend themselves to evil deeds'; remove the Jewish slaughter houses, because 'the butchers with their blood stains are common sights which . . . brutalize ignorant natures'; above all, hit the immoral greed of the landlords - 'vice can afford to pay more than honesty, but its profits at last go to landlords.'

They buried him just before the Great War in the churchyard of St Jude's; like the tenements he despised, now long demolished.

General William Booth promised 'Heaven in East London for everyone' and did his damndest to achieve it. The son of a Nottinghamshire builder, Booth was bought up in the fiery traditions of the Chartist Feargus O'Connor and the American Evangelist James Caughey. He first preached on the Quaker burial ground of the Mile End Waste and waged war on poverty. Warm, kind and simple, he won friends everywhere, preaching in penny gaffs and skittle alleys, wherever the poor collected. He leased the People's Market in Whitechapel Road and gave bread and soup to the poor for a penny; the destitute got it for nothing.

With his wild white hair and beard, his charismatic style and his army frock coat, the 'General' was a latter day Ignatius Loyola, marshalling his troops to do battle against indifference, greed and oppression. By 1878 his followers called themselves the Salvation Army and their women were the 'saviours of the slums'. Unlike Jack London, Booth wrote and spoke openly about prostitution, then a taboo subject in polite society.

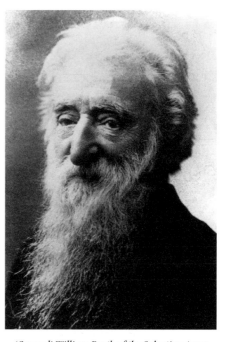

'General' William Booth of the Salvation Army saved souls and sinners in the Abyss.

> The profession of a prostitute is the only career in which the maximum is paid to the newest apprentice . . . and when once the poor girl has consented to buy the right to earn her living by the sacrifice of her virtue, then she is treated as a slave and an outcast by the very men who ruined her.

Frederick Charrington, brewery-owner turned saviour had a black book of brothel-keepers.

His 'Sally Army girls' set up a headquarters in the aptly named Angel Alley and they died young, sharing the hardships with the people of the Abyss.

The oddest philanthropist of the East End was Frederick Charrington and I am astonished that no one from the loonier ranks of Ripperologists has fingered him as Jack before now. The son of the extraordinarily rich firm of brewers, he was educated at Marlborough before going on the Grand Tour. Something of a rebel, Charrington turned to teetotalism. He also took to a tour far less grand - he wandered the streets of the Abyss. Outside one of his father's pubs, the Rising Sun, he saw a sight he would never forget. A wife was being beaten to a pulp by her husband:

> I looked up and saw my own name in high gilt letters . . . and it suddenly flashed into my mind that that was only one case of dreadful misery and fiendish brutality in one of the several hundred public houses that our firm possessed.

Two years before the Ripper, he had set up his headquarters on the Mile End Waste, in the wake of Booth, providing coffee rooms, a library and buildings for the YMCA, the YWCA and the Band of Hope. Like the Liberal giant William Gladstone (himself nominated recently as a potential Ripper), Charrington personally interviewed scores of prostitutes and their clients. He often had to be rescued by patrolling officers of H Division from a severe beating. In 1887 he launched an all-out attack on brothels, making lists of visitors to houses of ill-repute. His biographer, G. Thorne, wrote in 1912:

> bullies, the keepers of evil houses, the horrible folk who battened on shame and enriched themselves with the wages of sin, feared Frederick Charrington as they feared no policeman, no inspector, no other living being . . . the blackest scoundrels in London trembled both at his footsteps and his name.

If the police didn't for a moment consider Charrington as a possible Whitechapel murderer, then perhaps his little black book of brothel visitors should have been consulted by them. But perhaps he was too well known - his photograph was posted up in every bordello in the East End and he hired ex-cons and ex-drunks like Henry Holloway and 'Hellfire Tom' to convert the jeering crowds with their brimstone. By 1888, he had closed down nearly 200 brothels and their wayward inmates were cared for in Lady Ashburton's mansion.

The Ripper walked past this bollard in Commercial Street a thousand times on his nightly ramblings.

The converted wore enamel badges on their lapels with the initials BROTA - the 'blue ring of total abstinence'. Only the Abyss could create an oddity like Frederick Charrington.

I have tried here to capture the atmosphere of the Abyss in the Autumn of Terror as we follow in the footsteps of its most famous denizen - and his victims. Let us, like the writer William J. Fishman, imagine the scene:

> Even now, in the still hours, as the moon strikes the steeple of old Christ Church and casts a long shadow over the rickety tenements of Spitalfields, a sudden catch of movement, crouched silhouette in a desolate alleyway, all senses alert, as Old Jack, poised momentarily en route, continues on his way to a rendezvous with murder in the City of Dreadful Night.

DOUBLY UNFORTUNATE

POLLY NICHOLS

ANNIE CHAPMAN

LIZ STRIDE

KATE EDDOWES

MARY KELLY

RIP

1888

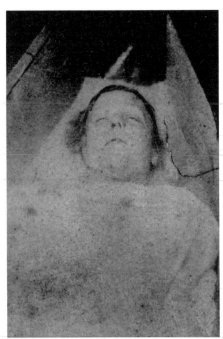

Mary Anne Nichols, known as Polly, died 30/31 August 1888.

VICTIM 1

MARY ANN NICHOLS - 'POLLY'

Mary Ann Nichols, nicknamed Polly, was forty-five at the time of her death. She was 5ft 2ins tall, with five teeth missing, mostly at the front, giving her otherwise delicate features a rather gormless expression. Her forehead had been scarred in childhood and her eyes were grey. Despite the dissolute lifestyle she had eventually adopted, Polly was described as 'a very clean woman' and the police surgeon who examined her naked corpse was surprised at the cleanliness of her thighs. The only photograph of her shows her in her coffin in Whitechapel Mortuary, a sheet used to cover her body. Her hair is plastered to her head, her lips slightly apart, her eyelids still open. The quality of the photograph is poor and only some lacerations to her right jaw give a hint of the ghastly mutilations under the cloth.

Polly was the daughter of Edward Walker, a locksmith-turned-blacksmith who, like many of the flotsam of the East End, moved around a great deal. At the age of nineteen, Polly married William Nichols, a printer, and they lived first in Bouverie Street at the hub of London's newspaper trade and then at Peabody Buildings, Stanford Street, Lambeth, just over Blackfriars Bridge. The marriage took place in the 'printers' church' of St Bride's, Fleet Street.

Polly gave birth to five children between 1866 and 1879 - Edward, Percy, Alice, Eliza and Henry. Not untypically for large families caught up in the economic miseries of the Great Depression, the Nichols argued. The eldest boy went to live with his grandfather and only his mother's murder persuaded him to talk to his father again. William eloped briefly with a midwife and Polly took to drink. Between 1877 and 1880 she left home at least five times, and by this time, the marriage had broken down completely. Each blamed the other - Polly for her husband's extramarital affair and William for her drinking. He paid her an allowance of five shillings a week and had custody of all the children except Edward. Only in 1882, when he learned she was living on immoral earnings, did the payments cease. The summons she brought against him was thrown out when her prostitution became known.

From 1880 until her death, we have an excellent record of Polly Nichols' lifestyle and whereabouts. Apart from a month in the spring of 1883 when she lived with her father in Camberwell, she was in and out of Lambeth Workhouse or Infirmary. Here, like many women of her class, she would not need the price of a bed for the night required by the dosshouses of Flower and Dean Street. She would be given a cold bath and her own clothes would be stashed away for safekeeping, along with any personal possessions she may have had. A day dress and pinafore of coarse cloth would have been given to her and she would have spent her days picking oakum or sewing mailbags until she was allowed out to look for work again. We know that she appeared at her brother's funeral in June 1886 and by that time was living with a blacksmith named Thomas Drew, whose forge was in York Road, Walworth. They must have quarrelled, because at the end of 1887 Polly was living rough in Trafalgar Square.

This had been the scene of 'Bloody Sunday', the clash between unskilled workers and the authorities, and it was regularly patrolled by the police. Polly was moved on and drifted from Lambeth to the Mitcham Workhouse at Holborn. For a brief period in the spring and early summer of 1888, she worked for Samuel and Sarah Cowdrey at their house in Rose Hill Road, Wandsworth. He was a Clerk of Works in the Police Department and in a letter Polly wrote to her father, she describes her employers as 'teetotallers and very religious'. She adds, with heavy irony, 'so I ought to get on'! Fond of the Cowdreys as Polly seemed to be and happy with her 'newly done up' surroundings, she stole clothes worth £3 10s and left.

By the August of 1888, Polly Nichols had been drawn into the teeming vice of Whitechapel. For most of that month, she shared a room at a dosshouse at 18 Thrawl Street with four other women. The rent was 4d a night and her bed-mate was Ellen Holland, known as Nelly. It was Ellen who was the last person to see Polly alive and she formally identified her body in the mortuary.

The last week in August saw Polly at the mixed-sex dosshouse at 56 Flower and Dean Street, known as the White House. It was from here that she went to her death.

COUNTDOWN TO MURDER

THURSDAY 30 / FRIDAY 31 AUGUST 1888

11.30 p.m.   Polly Nichols was seen walking by herself in Whitechapel Road.

12.30 a.m.   She left the Frying Pan public house on the corner of Thrawl Street and Brick Lane.

| 1.20 a.m. | Arrived at 18 Thrawl Street (200 yards away), merrily drunk. The deputy refused to admit her as she didn't have the 4d for the bed. 'I'll soon get my doss money,' she chuckled, 'See what a jolly bonnet I've got now.' |
| 2.30 a.m. approx. | Ellen Holland was on her way back from watching the second of two fires that night. |

G.R. Sims might have watched too:

> A great fire is a free sight which generally occurs in the night time; but a fire even at dead of night will attract gigantic crowds. When the news of it is spread by some mysterious means the streets are quickly filled with hurrying pedestrians anxious not to miss the spectacle. You will meet men and women at two and three in the morning running along and dressing as they go. All are hastening in one direction, that in which the sky is red with the reflection of the leaping flames.

At the end of an unusually wet summer, a conflagration had broken out in the engineering firm of Gibbs and Company in Shadwell Dry Dock. The blaze spread quickly to the adjacent Gowland's Coal Wharf and it wasn't put out until late the next morning. Polly met Ellen at the corner of Brick Lane and Osborn Street, saying that she had earned her doss-money three times over, but had spent it. She would not go back with Ellen to Thrawl Street, but wandered off in the direction of 'Flowery Dean' where she could sleep with a man. She was signing her death warrant.

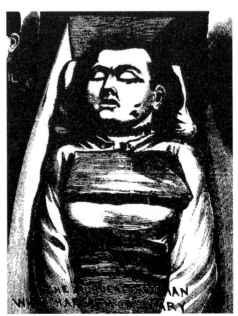

The corpse of Polly Nichols according to the artist of the Illustrated Police News. For all the likenesses are probably not good and the presentation rather catchpenny, artists' impressions of the murder sites are surprisingly accurate.

VICTIM 2

ANNIE CHAPMAN - 'DARK ANNIE'

The only known photograph of the Ripper's second victim shows a heavy-faced middle aged woman with thick lips, pale eyebrows and tightly curled hair. Like Polly Nichols, she had several teeth missing from her lower jaw. Dental neglect and poor diet made this a regular feature among the people of the Abyss. She was thickset, 5ft tall and had blue eyes. The post mortem (carried out shortly before or after the mortuary photograph was taken) revealed that she was malnourished and had in fact been dying from lung and brain membrane disease.

Annie Chapman. known as Dark Annie, died 8 September, 1888.

Eliza Ann Smith was born in Paddington in 1841, about a year before her parents married. Her father George was a trooper in the Life Guards and this explains the fact that the family lived in Windsor from 1856. 'To go for a soldier' was still regarded by many as a shameful thing in the 1840s when George married Ruth Chapman, but the Life Guards had a better reputation than most regiments because of their association with royalty. Army families, however had a rough time of it. Barracks had no married quarters, merely a blanket strung across a rope around a bed in a dormitory; these dormitories were acrid with the stench of ammonia from the stables below.

On May 1 1869, when the girl was already twenty-eight (quite elderly by 19th century working class standards), she married John Chapman at All Saints' Church, Knightsbridge. Chapman was a head coachman and related in some way to Annie's mother. In 1870 they lived first in Bayswater, then near Berkeley Square, these salubrious addresses linked of course with Chapman's jobs. He may have lost one of these because of Annie's propensity for lying and petty theft. The three children born of the marriage were sickly. In an age of very high infant mortality, one daughter died in 1882 and the son remained crippled all his life.

The family had now moved to St Leonard's Mill Farm Cottage, Windsor, where Chapman worked for Josiah Weeks. By the time of their daughter's death, however, the marriage had collapsed. The blame was placed squarely on Annie, described as 'drunken and immoral', but since John Chapman died four years later of cirrhosis of the liver, one wonders about the accuracy of this. He paid Annie ten shillings a week until he died.

For the four years after the breakdown of the marriage, Annie lived by her wits. She sold crocheted shawls, flowers and matches in the East End and became an occasional prostitute. By 1886, she was living with Jack Sievey or Sivvy, a sieve-maker, whose real name

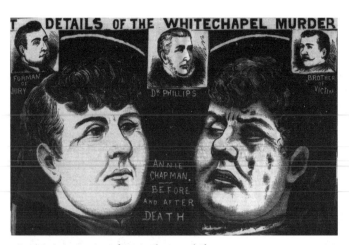

An artist's impression of Annie Chapman before and after her death. Most of the bruising to the face of the corpse was caused by her fight with a dosshouse inmate days before she died.

is unknown. Most of her friends knew her as Annie Sievey, though no actual marriage seems to have taken place. By the May of 1888 she had left Sievey's house at 30 Dorset Street and had moved into Crossingham's Lodging House across the road, opposite Miller's Court where the last of the Ripper's victims was to die.

Friends of Annie made light of her drinking, but her temper was in no doubt. In the first week in September she received a black eye and other bruises from another prostitute, Eliza Cooper, the brawl starting in Crossingham's and continuing in the taproom of the Britannia public house on the corner of Dorset Street and Commercial Street. The cause is not certain, but it involved the theft of two shillings and another Crossingham lodger, 'Harry the Hawker', one of the countless down-and-outs of the Abyss known only by their nicknames.

COUNTDOWN TO MURDER

FRIDAY 7 / SATURDAY 8 SEPTEMBER 1888

11.30 p.m.	Annie was admitted to the kitchen of Crossingham's by the deputy warden, Timothy Donovan.
12.12 a.m.	Fellow-lodger William Stevens, a printer, saw Annie, still in the kitchen, put two tablets into a torn envelope on the mantelpiece and return it to her pocket. He noticed that the envelope carried the feather and garter crest of the Sussex regiment and a London postmark.
12.30 a.m.	Frederick Stevens (no relation of William), another Crossingham lodger, drank a pint of beer with Annie. Exactly where this was he didn't say.
1.35 a.m.	Annie went back to Crossingham's where Donovan found her munching a baked potato. She couldn't afford the 4d for the night. 'I haven't got it,' she told him, still nursing her bruised face and ribs. 'I am weak and ill and have been in the infirmary. Don't let the bed. I'll be back soon.'

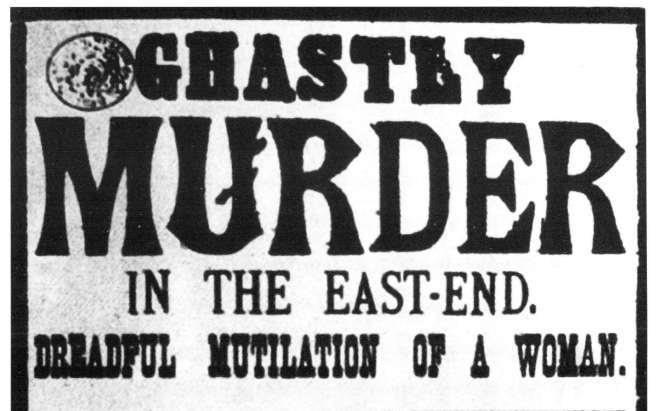

GHASTLY MURDER

IN THE EAST-END.

DREADFUL MUTILATION OF A WOMAN.

Capture : Leather Apron

Another murder of a character even more diabolical than that perpetrated in Back's Row, on Friday week, was discovered in the same neighbourhood, on Saturday morning. At about six o'clock a woman was found lying in a back yard at the foot of a passage leading to a lodging-house in a Old Brown's Lane, Spitalfields. The house is occupied by a Mrs. Richardson, who lets it out to lodgers, and the door which admits to this passage, at the foot of which lies the yard where the body was found, is always open for the convenience of lodgers. A lodger named Davis was going down to work at the time mentioned and found the woman lying on her back close to the flight of steps leading into the yard. Her throat was cut in a fearful manner. The woman's body had been completely ripped open and the heart and other organs laying about the place, and portions of the entrails round the victim's neck. An excited crowd gathered in front of Mrs. Richardson's house and also round the mortuary in old Montague Street, whither the body was quickly conveyed. As the body lies in the rough coffin in which it has been placed in the mortuary · the same coffin in which the unfortunate Mrs. Nicholls was first placed · it presents a fearful sight. The body is that of a woman about 45 years of age. The height is exactly five feet. The complexion is fair, with wavy brown hair; the eyes are blue, and two lower teeth have been knocked out. The nose is rather large and prominent.

Posters like these appeared all over the Abyss.

1.40 a.m. approx.	Old John 'Brummy' Evans saw Annie making for Little Paternoster Row towards Brushfield Street. 'I won't be long, Brummy,' she called to him. 'Make sure Tim keeps the bed for me.'
5.30 a.m. approx.	Elizabeth Darrell, also known as Elizabeth Long, reported seeing Annie Chapman standing on the pavement outside Number 29, Hanbury Street talking to a man, a little taller than she was, who looked 'foreign'. The word was usually a euphemism for Jewish. She heard him ask 'Will you?' and Annie said 'Yes.'

That may have been the last word she spoke.

Elizabeth Stride, known as Long Liz, died 29/30 September 1888. Alone of the Ripper's victims, she was not mutilated. Her crushed lower lip was the result of an old accident.

VICTIM 3

ELIZABETH STRIDE - 'LONG LIZ'

The Ripper's third victim was Elizabeth Stride, born in 1843 to Gustaf Ericson and his wife Beata Carlsdottir of Stora Tumlehed, Torslanda, Sweden. According to the custom of Scandinavian countries, the baby was officially Elizabeth Gustafsdottir. The only known photograph of her is the one taken in the mortuary. It shows a calm face with tangled hair and a disfigured mouth. There is little to match the description of her from Constable Walter Dew of H Division, who said 'traces of prettiness remained in her face and there must have been a time when she was exceedingly proud of her curly black hair.' The mortuary photograph was not rediscovered until 1988 and it does at least hint at fine bone structure. Her body is covered in a dark blanket and only the most superficial cuts are visible to the right side of her neck. All the teeth were missing from her left lower jaw.

In 1860, Elizabeth, then seventeen, moved to Carl Johan, Gothenburg, to work as a servant. Two years later we find her in the neighbouring parish of the Cathedral, but by 1865 she was described as a prostitute, had given birth to a daughter who was stillborn, and had been treated for venereal disease. In 1866, for reasons which are unknown, she moved to London. She may have been in service in a house near Hyde Park until her marriage in 1869 to John Stride at the church of St Giles-in-the-Field. The marriage lines give her name as Gustafson, a misspelling of the slightly anglicized form. She was then living in Gower Street. John was a ship's carpenter but turned his hand to running a coffee shop in Upper North Street and the High Street, Poplar between 1870 and 1874. The business did not succeed. At least one of the pair was in Poplar workhouse in the spring of 1877.

A probable case of mistaken identity occurred when the steamer *Princess Alice* sank off Woolwich. Accidents on the Thames were common - it was one of the busiest waterways in the world - and the *Alice* was in collision with a collier, the *Bywell Castle,* in September 1878. Both captains seem to have been to blame for carelessness and poor navigation, but the *Alice* suffered far more, with between 600 and 700 passengers drowned. Many of their bodies were found washed up on the river reaches days later. Some of these were laid out in Woolwich Town Hall for relatives to identify.

The wreck of the Princess Alice - the worst river disaster on the Thames and the one in which Liz Stride claimed to have damaged her mouth and lost her husband. Neither claim was true.

When Elizabeth Stride died in the 'Autumn of Terror', several papers, anxious to glean every known fact about her, claimed that she was the same Elizabeth Stride who had worked on the *Princess Alice* and had claimed that her husband and children had died in the accident. This was a story that she herself told friends, even explaining that her twisted lip was caused by the boot heel of a man clambering out of danger as the steamer keeled over. Nothing about this story fits. Stride did not work for the London Steamboat Company, as his wife claimed; the couple were childless and John Stride died in Bromley Sick Asylum in 1884 from a heart attack. The post mortem on Elizabeth revealed that the hard palate she had said was smashed in the accident was still intact. It seems likely that Mrs Stride enjoyed the notoriety of being an alien in London. The East End was full of foreigners, but they were largely Eastern European Jews. A Swede was different and tall tales may have been 'Long Liz's' stock-in-trade. Her English accent was impeccable and, perhaps oddly, she was fluent in Yiddish.

Like the Ripper's first two victims, Liz Stride's marriage had broken down for some time before she met her death. By 1881 she was admitted to Whitechapel workhouse - the Spike - with bronchitis and the following year she was living in a common lodging house at 32 Flower and Dean Street. Three years later we find her in Dorset Street with Michael Kidney, a labourer seven years her junior. Kidney had a police record, and was known as a bully and drinker, beating Liz up from time to time and varying in his behaviour towards her to the extent that he often had no idea where she was and once tried to padlock her in the house!

In 1887-8 Liz asked for financial support from the Swedish Church off the Ratcliffe Highway, still notorious as the 'most dangerous street in England'. In the same period, she was prosecuted no less than eight times for drunkenness, and on one occasion may have used the alias of Annie Fitzgerald; why is not

An artist's impression of Long Liz.

clear, as she was obviously well known to the constables who shared her beat.

By September 1888, Liz was back at 32 Flower and Dean Street where Dr Barnardo spoke to her. He recognized 'Long Liz' later on the marble slab. This chance encounter has led to Ripperologists pointing an accusatory finger at him.

COUNTDOWN TO MURDER

SATURDAY 29 / SUNDAY 30 SEPTEMBER 1888

6.30 p.m.	Liz visited the Queen's Head public house on the corner of Commercial and Fashion Street, where she had often been drunk and disorderly.
7.00 p.m.	She returned to 32 Flower and Dean Street and borrowed a clothes brush from fellow-lodger Charles Preston, a barber. She then left a piece of velvet cloth with another lodger, Catherine Lane, a charwoman.
11.00 p.m.	Two labourers, John Gardner and J. Best (his Christian name is not recorded), saw Liz leaving the Bricklayers' Arms in Settles Street with a man who was definitely British and had the appearance of a clerk. There was a sudden downpour and Best and Gardner playfully shouted a warning to Liz - 'That's Leather Apron getting round you.' Long Liz wore a flower in her dress now and the couple walked off in the Commercial Road direction.
11.45 p.m.	Labourer William Marshall undoubtedly saw the same man with Liz outside his house at 64 Berner Street. He heard him say 'You would say anything but your prayers.' The couple walked on in the direction of Dutfield's Yard.
Midnight approx.	Fruiterer Matthew Packer (although he vehemently denied it to the press later) sold half a pound of grapes to the man with Liz. The couple stood in the rain for almost half

an hour across the road from his shop, at the entrance to Dutfield's Yard.

12.30 a.m.   The couple were still there when Constable 424H William Smith reached that part of his beat.

12.45 a.m.   Labourer James Brown saw a couple who may have been Liz and her client leaning up against the wall of the Board School in Fairclough Street. 'Not tonight,' she was saying, 'Maybe some other night.' It is very possible that this is a wrong sighting, because Israel Schwartz, a Jewish Hungarian immigrant, had a different story to tell. He was going home along Berner Street when he saw Liz Stride being thrown to the ground by the man she was with. He crossed the street and 'Long Liz's' assailant shouted 'Lipski' at him, almost certainly an anti-Semitic expletive relating to a Jew of the same name recently hanged for murder. Schwartz was then aware of a second man lighting his pipe nearby and, fearing a mugging, ran.

As he did so, he left Liz Stride to the Ripper.

VICTIM 4

CATHARINE EDDOWES - KATE

The fourth Ripper victim was the second in one night, creating what has come to be known in Ripperology as 'the double event'. The police photograph shows a long-haired woman whose face has been badly mutilated. Unlike the mortuary photographs of Polly Nichols, Annie Chapman and 'Long Liz' Stride, Catharine Eddowes' naked body is entirely on display, propped up as was the custom for photographing corpses in the American West, the telltale zig-zag stitches of the police surgeon running from abdomen to throat. The lacerations to the face make any attempt at an accurate description of the woman impossible. She was forty-six years old at the time of her murder.

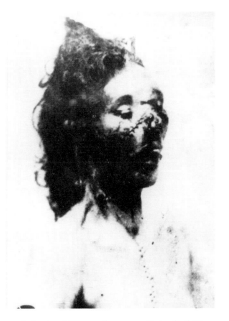

Catherine Eddowes, known as Kate, died 30 September, 1888. She was the second victim of the 'double event'.

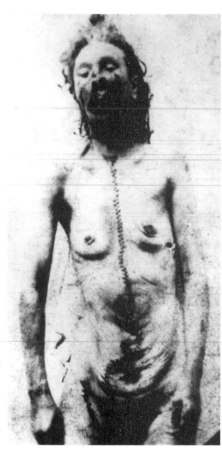

Kate Eddowes stitched up by the police surgeon prior to burial.

Kate was born in Wolverhampton. Her father George was a tinplate worker who moved with his family to Bermondsey in 1843 or 1844. Before her mother's death (Catharine Eddowes senior died in 1855), little Kate attended St John's Charity School in Tooley Street, not far from the river. After this, most of her brothers and sisters went into the Bermondsey Workhouse (the Victorian equivalent of being taken into care). It is possible that Kate returned to Wolverhampton to live with an aunt, but between 1861 and 1863 she went to live with Thomas Conway, also known as Thomas Quinn, who was receiving a pension from the army, having served in the 18th Foot. In the 1860s, Conway wrote chapbooks which he and Kate sold in Birmingham and elsewhere. It is unlikely they were married and between 1865 and 1873 three children were born.

By 1880 the common law marriage was over, each blaming the other in a reflection of the Nichols marriage. According to her daughter Annie, who seems to have led an altogether more sober life than her mother, Kate's heavy drinking was the cause. Others held Conway to blame, because teetotaller though he was, he apparently beat Kate on a regular basis.

In 1881 Kate moved in with John Kelly, an Irish market porter who lodged in Flower and Dean Street. 'Quiet and inoffensive' with 'sharp, intelligent eyes', Kelly became progressively more ill through the 1880s, suffering from kidney trouble. Unlike many East End relationships, there is no record of discord between the pair.

Kate's daughter Annie married Louis Phillips and the young couple seem to have kept on the move to avoid Kate's scrounging.

In common with many East Enders, Kate and John Kelly picked hops in Kent in the September of 1888. Hop-picking was a literal breath of fresh air for the people of the Abyss. It was a paid working holiday and vast improvement over their meagre existence in the courts and alleyways of home. The couple's return on September 28 saw them split up, probably because of economic necessity. Kate slept in the Shoe Lane Workhouse while Kelly went to Cooney's Lodging House in Thrawl Street.

'I have come back,' Kate said to the deputy, 'to earn the reward offered for the apprehension of the Whitechapel murderer. I think I know him.' When the deputy urged her to take care that she shouldn't become a victim, she said 'No fear of that.'

COUNTDOWN TO MURDER

SATURDAY 29 / SUNDAY 30 SEPTEMBER 1888

8.00 a.m.   Kate joined John Kelly at the Shoe Lane

Workhouse and she took a pair of his boots to a pawn shop in Church St, where she received 2/6. She gave the name Jane Kelly and was given a ticket.

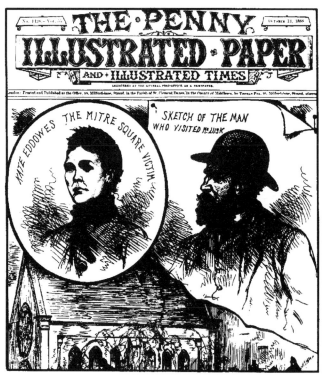

'The Mitre Square Victim' according to a contemporary artist.

10-11 a.m.   With the cash, the couple bought tea and sugar and had breakfast at Cooney's Lodging House in Thrawl Street.

2.00 p.m.   Broke again, Kate left Kelly in Houndsditch, intending to borrow money from her daughter in Bermondsey. She didn't find her.

8.30 p.m.   Kate was found by Constable 31 Louis Robinson of the City Force lying drunk on the pavement outside 29 Aldgate High Street, surrounded by a small crowd. He stood her up, but she slumped down again and together with Constable George Simons, they bundled her off to Bishopsgate Police Station.

8.50 p.m.   Having given her name as 'Nothing', she was locked in a cell by the desk man, Sergeant James Byfield and was sleeping shortly afterwards.

12.15 a.m.   Kate had woken up and was singing to herself.

12.30 a.m.   She asked to be released and Constable George Hutt told her that that wouldn't happen until she was 'capable'. 'I can do that now,' she told him.

1.00 a.m.   Hutt released Kate. She asked him the time. 'Too late for you to get any more drink,' he told her. 'I shall get a damned fine hiding when I get home,' she said. She gave her name as Mary Ann Kelly (curiously similar to that of the last Ripper victim) and her address as 6 Fashion Street. At the door, she said, 'All right. Good night, old cock.'

| 1.35 a.m. | Kate was seen in the entrance to Church Passage, which led to Mitre Square, talking to a man. She had a hand on his chest. This sighting was made by three men, Joseph Lawende, a cigarette salesman; Harry Harris, a furniture dealer; and Joseph Levy, a butcher, all of whom were on their way home from the Imperial Club down the road. |

Whoever the man was with Kate Eddowes is highly likely to have been Jack the Ripper.

VICTIM 5

MARY JANE KELLY - 'BLACK MARY' 'FAIR EMMA' 'GINGER'

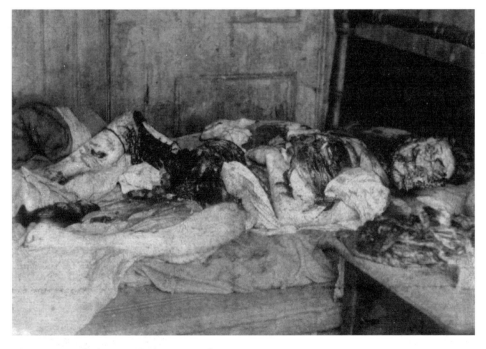

Mary Jane Kelly, known as 'Fair Emma' and 'Ginger', died 9 November 1888. The remains of her chemise (petticoat) can clearly be seen on her left shoulder and the supposed letter 'M' daubed in blood on the wall behind her bed.

Like many East End women, and three of the Ripper's other victims, Mary Kelly used aliases. She occasionally called herself Marie Jeanette, giving rise to a possible French connection, but was also known, extremely confusingly, as 'Black Mary', 'Fair Emma' and 'Ginger'! We have no clear idea of what Mary Kelly looked like, as the only photograph of her is the infamous one taken in situ in her room at 13 Miller's Court after the Ripper had carried out the most revolting mutilations of all. There is little left of her face. It has become the norm to describe her as attractive, probably because she was younger than the other victims by eighteen or nineteen years (she was twenty-four when she died). Among the myths with which Ripperologists have had to contend for many years was that Mary Kelly was pregnant. The recently-found post mortem report makes it clear that she was not.

Much of Mary's early life is only known through stories she told friends in and around Whitechapel and no supporting evidence has come to light. She claimed to have been born in 1863, daughter of John Kelly, a labourer in County Limerick, Ireland. When she was very young, the family moved either to Caernarvon or Carmarthen, where John worked in an iron foundry. This move is very much in keeping with the immigrant Irish, unable to cope in the depressed atmosphere of post-famine Ireland. In 1879, Mary married a miner called Davies, who was killed in a pit accident in 1881 or 1882. She drifted into prostitution in Cardiff, and came to London in 1884. Whether, as she claimed, she found employment in a West End brothel and spent a while as a courtesan in Paris, or whether this was a tall tale typical of those told by people with an unverifiable past, we shall never know. It is possible that she worked as a domestic servant in the mid 1880s, perhaps spending some time at the Providence Row Night Refuge in Crispin Street, Spitalfields. She moved around considerably in this period, lodging at St George's Street, off the Ratcliffe Highway and living with a man named Morganstone in Stepney. She lodged with a Mrs Buki (possibly a misspelling) and a Mrs Carthy before taking up with a plasterer, Joseph Fleming, who lived in Bethnal Green, sometime in 1886.

The April of 1887 found her living in Cooney's Lodging House in Thrawl Street, where she met Joseph Barnett on April 8, Good Friday. Barnett was a labourer and porter at Billingsgate and the couple moved in together at various lodgings - George Street, Little Paternoster Row and 13 Miller's Court, off Dorset Street. The rent here was 4s 6d a week and Mary Kelly owed £1 10s by the time of her murder.

Mary drank occasionally and appeared to be more afraid than most of her working contemporaries of the Whitechapel killings. By October 30, Barnett had left her, probably because she invited other working girls to stay in her tiny room. One of these was a Mrs Maria Harvey, a laundress who 'frequented' (i.e. solicited in) the Aldgate area. The other was a German (Dutch?) girl, probably Julia van Turney who lived at 1 Miller's Court.

COUNTDOWN TO MURDER

THURSDAY 8 / FRIDAY 9 NOVEMBER 1888

Early evening, Mary was in the company of Lizzie Allbrook, a younger friend who was not a prostitute.

7.30-8.00 p.m.   The pair were visited by Joseph Barnett, in friendly mood.

Mary Kelly entering her tiny room at 13 Miller's Court. The building, with its broken window pane is extraordinarily accurate.

11.00 p.m.	Mary was possibly seen in The Britannia public house with a young man. It is also possible that either before or after this (common sense would indicate before) she was seen with Barnett and Julia in the Horn of Plenty on the corner of Crispin and Dorset Streets.
11.45 p.m.	Mary Cox, a widow and prostitute from 5 Miller's Court, saw Mary, drunk, in the company of a man with a blotchy face, carrotty moustache and billycock hat. He was carrying a pail of beer.
12-1.00 a.m.	Several witnesses, including Catharine Pickett of Miller's Court, heard Mary singing 'Only a violet I plucked from my mother's grave'.
2.00 a.m.	George Hutchinson, an unemployed labourer who lodged in Commercial Street, was approached by Mary, who knew him, and she asked him to lend her 6d. As Hutchinson was broke, he had to turn her down. As she walked towards Aldgate a man approached her and he heard laughter and snatches of conversation. 'You will be alright,' he said to her, 'for what I have told you.' And he put his arm around her shoulders. The man carried a parcel, wrapped with string, but Hutchinson couldn't see the man's face even when the pair stopped under a street light outside the Queen's Head. He followed them to Miller's Court. 'Alright, my dear,' he heard Mary say, 'Come along, you will be comfortable.' She kissed him and Hutchinson noticed that he gave her a red handkerchief as she said she had lost hers. After 45 minutes, Hutchinson left the area.
3.45 a.m. approx	Three residents or visitors at Miller's Court - Sarah Lewis, Mrs Kennedy and Elizabeth Prater - all heard a scream of 'Oh, Murder!' from the direction of Number 13. That was probably the last word Mary Kelly ever spoke.

JUST FOR JOLLY

The next job I do I shall clip the ladies ears off and send to the police officers just for jolly wouldn't you.

JUST FOR JOLLY

The mechanics of murder do not make pretty reading, but the modus operandi of a serial killer fascinates millions, and it did in Victorian England as much as it does today. The wielding of a knife, the direction of an attack, the exact nature of mutilation tell us a great deal about the fiend who walked the East End.

The first of the Ripper sites - Durward Street prior to demolition in the 1960s. Polly Nichols' body was found by the garage doors on the left.

What exactly happened to Polly Nichols? At about twenty to four in the morning of Friday August 31, two carmen, Charles Cross and Robert Paul, were on their way to work, walking along Buck's Row. One of the more incredible facts about the Ripper murders is that because of the lifestyle of the people of the Abyss, there was never any time in each twenty-four hours when the streets were totally deserted. Cross saw what he thought was a piece of tarpaulin lying in the gutter opposite the manager's house at Essex Wharf. Closer inspection revealed that it was the body of a woman, her skirts hitched up around her hips. Paul thought she was still alive - 'I think she's breathing, but it's very little if she is.' The fact that the woman's hands were cold would indicate that she was probably already dead. The carmen left her there and went in search of a patrolling policeman.

Constable 55H James Mizen was on his beat in nearby Hanbury Street when Cross and Paul found him about 4.15 a.m. While the three were hurrying back to Buck's Row, Constable 97J John Neil had also stumbled on Polly Nichols' corpse. Neil signalled with his bull's eye lantern to Constable 96J John Thain, who joined him. Neil seems to have been the senior man and he sent Thain to fetch Dr Llewellyn, the local police surgeon, and Mizen, who had also arrived by this time to fetch an ambulance (a wheeled stretcher which was also used to carry drunks).

Rees Llewellyn LRCP was woken at his surgery home in the Whitechapel Road and made his way with Thain to Buck's Row. He pronounced Polly Nichols dead and her body was taken by Sergeant Kerby of J Division to the Old Montague Street mortuary. By the time the most senior officer, Inspector John Spratling, arrived, local lad James Green, who lived at New Cottage nearby, was washing the blood off the cobblestones.

Today the precise details of a post mortem examination would never be reported in the newspapers. While most people would think (wrongly) that we now live in a more violent society and that the media use more licence than ever before, it's unlikely that any daily of today would go as far as the *Times* did in early September 1888:

> Five of the teeth are missing [no connection with the murder] and there was a slight laceration of the tongue. There was a bruise running along the lower part of the jaw on the right side of the face. That might have been caused by a blow from a fist or pressure from a thumb. There was a circular bruise on the left side of the face, which also might have been inflicted by the pressure of the fingers. On the left side of the neck, about 1 inch below the jaw, there was an incision about 4 in. in length and ran from a point immediately below the ear. On the same side, but an inch below, and commencing about 1 in. in front of it, was a circular incision, which terminated at a point about 3 in. below the right jaw. That incision completely severed all the tissues down to the vertebrae. The large vessels of the neck on both sides were severed. The incision was about 8 in. in length. The cuts must have been caused by a long-bladed knife, moderately sharp and used with great violence. No blood was found on the breast, either of the body or the clothes. There were no injuries about the body until just about the lower part of the abdomen. Two or three inches from the left side was a wound running in a jagged manner. The wound was a very deep one and the tissues were cut through. There were several incisions running across the abdomen. There were also three or four similar cuts running downwards, on the right side, all of which had been caused by a knife which had been used violently and downwards. The injuries were from left to right and might have been done by a left-handed person. All the injuries had been caused by the same instrument.

Polly Nichols was identified by Mary Monk, a fellow inmate of Polly's from the Lambeth Workhouse. A routine check of the dead woman's clothes had uncovered a laundry mark of that institution. Contrary to the blowsily dressed floozies of the Hammer films, Polly wore her entire wardrobe and would be regarded as a virtual bag lady today. She wore an ulster overcoat with brass buttons, a brown linsey frock, a chest flannel, two petticoats, a pair of stays, a pair of black woollen stockings, a pair of men's boots and a black straw bonnet. All she carried in her pockets was a comb, a handkerchief and a broken mirror. Her friend Ellen Holland also identified her later; '. . . it was enough to make anybody shed a tear, sir,' she admitted at the inquest which followed.

Forensic science was in its infancy in 1888. It would be four years before Francis Galton perfected the fingerprinting technique and seventeen before a conviction was bought solely on fingerprinting evidence. Genetic fingerprinting - the comparison of DNA - was still a century away. There seems to be no comment by Llewellyn as to whether Polly had sex with her killer in Buck's Row or somewhere nearby. Traces of semen might have been discoverable in the circumstances, but Polly was a known prostitute and could have had several clients that night.

Despite the lack of forensic expertise - the great days of Spilsbury, Simpson, Camps and Cameron lay in the future - Llewellyn seems to have done a thorough job and his account is detailed and clear. The weapon used was long and moderately sharp. The relative lack of blood would indicate that the mutilations were carried out after death (although this and the lack of slashes in Polly's clothing have led some Ripperologists to surmise that she was killed naked elsewhere, redressed and dumped in Buck's Row). The killer may have been left-handed (and this was to spawn furious rows between medical experts in the months ahead). Most interesting is Llewellyn's comment on the bruising to the throat. Was Polly punched by the Ripper or strangled manually, or both? The police patrolled the end of Buck's Row every half an hour. A scuffle or struggle would surely have alerted their attention. That meant that if Polly was killed where she was found (and the weight of evidence suggests that she was) then the killer had little time in which to work. He may have knocked her down with a punch, throttled her into unconsciousness and then cut her throat before starting work on the mutilations. Of these, Llewellyn testified later at the inquest that the murderer 'must have had some rough anatomical knowledge for he seemed to have attacked all the vital parts'.

This is not actually true, because the heart - in fact the entire chest area - had been left severely alone. It gave rise however to one of the most enduring of the Ripper myths - that of the Mad Doctor.

Despite extensive police enquiries in the weeks that followed, Chief Inspector Donald Swanson said on October 19, the 'absence of motives which lead to violence and of any scrap of evidence either direct or circumstantial, left the police without the slightest shadow of a trace.'

The problem for the authorities is that they hadn't the faintest idea that they were dealing with a new kind of criminal - Jack the

Ripper was the world's first serial killer. It has taken us nearly a century to cope with people like him.

Polly Nichols was given a pauper's burial in the City of London Cemetery at Little Ilford, Essex on Thursday, September 6 1888, plucked from the obscurity of her life by death. They even wrote a song about her.

> And now poor Mary Nichols' death relating,
> In Buck's Row, Whitechapel, there did lie,
> While in the dark her body lay awaiting
> And no one there to see that poor soul die.

A little before six o'clock on the morning of Saturday, September 8, two days after Polly Nichols' funeral, John Davis, an old carman who worked at Leadenhall Market, went into the back yard of Number 29, Hanbury Street, where he lodged on the third floor with his wife and three sons. He hadn't been able to sleep and had lain awake between three and five before getting up at a quarter to six by the Christ Church clock.

At the top of the steps he could see below and to his left the body of a woman lying on her back between the steps and the yard fence. Her dress had been pulled up and her intestines had been draped over her left shoulder. Seventeen people lived at Number 29 and the passage that ran between the yard and Hanbury Street was soon

The second of the Ripper sites - No.29 Hanbury Street before its demolition in 1972. The alleyway to the yard at the back where Jack took his victim was reached by the door on the left.

full of them and curious passers-by. One of the first was Henry Holland, a young man on his way to work at Chiswell Street when Davis stopped him to tell him what he had found. Holland ran to Spitalfields Market but the constable there told him he could not leave his fixed point duty and refused to follow Holland. James Kent and James Green, also on their way to work, were also stopped by the probably hysterical Davis. Kent took a look at the body and got himself a stiff brandy from somewhere before he returned with a tarpaulin to cover it.

Inspector Joseph Chandler was on duty in Commercial Street Police Station that morning and he saw men running towards Hanbury Street. The first senior police officer on the scene, Chandler sent for the police surgeon, Dr Phillips, and for an ambulance. In time-honoured tradition he cleared the crowds away and supervised the covering of the body.

The yard at the back of No.29, showing the open door that linked the passageway to the street itself. It was a favourite haunt for prostitutes and their clients. Annie's body was found to the right of the steps as we look at them, her head pointing towards the house.

Dr George Bagster Phillips MRCS, who carried out or attended post mortems on four of the five Ripper victims.

Dr George Bagster Phillips was police surgeon to H Division. He was to be called to two more Ripper murder sites after this one and more than any other medical man, had an overview of the killer's M.O. He was fetched from his house in Spital Square and reached Hanbury Street at 6.30 a.m. He ordered the body to be taken to the Whitechapel Infirmary Mortuary in Eagle Street, where it was washed and laid out by two female attendants.

At the subsequent inquest into Annie Chapman's murder (she was identified by her friend, washerwoman Amelia Palmer at eleven thirty on the day of her death), Phillips gave his description of the body *in situ* and, in response to the coroner's questions, his professional opinion on various issues. The same knife was used on the throat gashes and the ghastly mutilations to the abdomen - it was very sharp and at least 6 inches long, probably longer - and he even speculated on the sort of man who had access to such knives: medical men (adding fuel to the Mad Doctor nonsense) and slaughtermen (unwittingly perhaps unleashing a potential pogrom against Jews of the Ghetto who slaughtered animals according to strict kosher ritual). Annie Chapman had been dead for at least two hours, possibly more, and a struggle must have taken place. Curious that John Davis, awake throughout this entire period, should have heard nothing.

Bagster Phillips carried out his post-mortem in what was actually a shed and both he and Wynne Baxter, the coroner, complained about its inadequacies. Some of the bruising to Annie's face was older, clearly the result of her fight with Eliza Cooper. Even so, the woman had apparently been pushed by her murderer too and the protruding tongue gave ample testimony to manual strangulation. The actual cause of death was syncope, a failure of the action of the heart caused by loss of blood when her throat was cut. The coroner's court was cleared of women and children on September 19 when Bagster Phillips was recalled to give detailed evidence of mutilation.

The *Lancet*, the surgeons' quarterly, gave the following précis:

> The abdomen had been entirely laid open: the intestines, severed from their mesenteric attachments, had been lifted out of the body and placed on the shoulder of the corpse; whilst from the pelvis, the uterus and its appendages with the upper portion of the vagina and the posterior two-thirds of the bladder, had been entirely removed. No trace of these parts could be found and the incisions were clearly cut, avoiding the rectum and dividing the vagina low enough to avoid injury to the cervix uteri.

If Polly Nichols' murder bought out morbidly curious sightseers, who collected in knots along Buck's and Baker's Rows or hung around the mortuary gates, Annie Chapman's killing sent shockwaves of panic throughout the Abyss. Experts now agree that Polly was the first victim of the man called Jack, but in the Autumn of Terror few members of the public or press made the connection. After all, there had been at least two gruesome murders of women earlier that year. On April 2 a prostitute named Emma Smith was assaulted by a gang of three youths who robbed her, raped her and thrust what was probably a broken bottle into her vagina. She died of peritonitis three days later in the London Hospital. The attack had taken place on the corner of Wentworth Street and Brick Lane, placing Emma in the Ripper's half mile. Police investigating the case believed the killers were members of a gang from the Nichol, a notorious no-go area at the northern end of Brick Lane, who preyed on prostitutes and acted as pimps from time to time. If Emma had been invading the patch of another 'unfortunate', perhaps this was their way of warning such trespassers off. The name of one such gang associated with East End violence was the Hoxton High Rips - a macabre twist.

In the early hours of August 7 (the day after Bank Holiday Monday) Martha Tabram, also known as Turner, met her death on the first floor landing of George Yard Buildings (Gunthorpe Street), probably at the hands of a Grenadier Guardsman who killed her with his bayonet. In those days, off-duty soldiers rarely had the cash for a suit of civilian clothes, so wore their scarlet 'walking out' dress instead. They probably carried their bayonets for protection in what was a notoriously dangerous part of London.

It is significant that Bagster Phillips was asked at Annie Chapman's inquest whether her wounds could have been administered with a bayonet. But neither the triangular-bladed infantry pattern nor the new conventional blade of 1887 could have caused Annie's mutilations.

Fear and eventual panic were growing in the Abyss. West End reporters mingled with the inhabitants of the Ghetto, reporting their clothes, their habits and their speech patterns as though they were some foreign species. 'Life ain't no great thing with many on us,' one woman told a reporter, 'But we don't all want to be murdered . . .'

The Victorian press, even more than now, was unconcerned with accuracy. Interestingly, its artists were good and the sketches of the buildings which form the backdrop to the 'ghastly finds' are quite accurate, judging by later photographs of the same premises. The reporters smelt blood along with everybody else. *The Star* was typical of the 'tabloids' of the day:

London lies today under the spell of a great terror. A nameless reprobate - half beast, half man - is at large, who is daily gratifying his murderous instincts on the most miserable and defenceless classes of the community . . . Hideous malice, deadly cunning, insatiable thirst for blood - all these are the marks of the mad homicide. The ghoul-like creature who stalks through the streets of London . . . is simply drunk with blood and he will have more.

The third Ripper site - Berner Street, off the Commercial Road. The entrance to Dutfield's Yard, where Liz Stride's body was found, is marked by the cartwheel on the wall. The large building was used by the International Workingmen's Club at the time of the murder.

He did. While good citizens, actually safe as houses in the West End, bombarded the police with complaints about incompetence and inactivity, while offers of rewards flooded in and demands for the resignation of the Home Secretary grew, Jack met Liz Stride.

At about one o'clock in the morning of Friday September 30, Louis Diemschütz, a street jewellery seller, was on his way back from a gruelling day at Westow Hill Market, Sydenham. The tobacconist's clock in Commercial Road had just struck the hour when he turned his pony and trap into the entrance to Dutfield's Yard along Berner Street. There was light and Yiddish singing spilling out of the International Workingmen's Educational Club to his right, but the pony shied and would not walk on. Diemschütz saw a bundle against the yard gates and prodded it with his whip. He got down and in the light of the match he struck saw what appeared to be a drunk. He went into the Club where his wife worked and he and fellow club member Morris Eagle and Isaacs Kozebrodsky returned to the bundle to find it was a woman whose throat had been cut. Two of them dashed off to find a policeman. In fact they met horse-keeper Edward Spooner chatting up a girl (probably a prostitute) outside the Beehive pub in Fairclough Street and all three came back to Dutfield's, apparently collecting Constable 252H Henry Lamb at the corner of Grove Street on the way. Lamb sent for help from the nearest station and another constable, whose name is not recorded, sent for Dr William Blackwell.

The doctor arrived at 1.16 a.m. by his watch and pronounced the woman dead, believing she had been that way for less than twenty minutes. The prevailing weight of evidence then is that

Diemschütz's arrival with the pony and trap had interrupted the Ripper at work. The minute or two it would have taken for Diemschütz to find Eagle and Kozebrodsky would have been enough for the killer to nip out of Dutfield's Yard in the half-darkness and make his way southwest in search of another victim.

Blackwell said later that the woman had probably been killed standing up, her throat exposed by her head being snapped back from behind. Bagster Phillips, who carried out the post-mortem, disagreed, continuing the problem of conflicting expert evidence which so bedevils the Whitechapel murders.

> The deceased [wrote Blackwell] was lying on her left side obliquely across the passage [the entrance to the yard], her face looking towards the right wall. Her legs were drawn up, her feet close against the wall of the right side of the passage . . . Her dress was unfastened at the neck. The neck and chest were quite warm, as were also the legs and the face was slightly warm. The hands were cold. The right hand was open and on the chest and was smeared in blood . . . The appearance of the face was quite placid. The mouth was slightly open . . . In the neck was a long incision which exactly corresponded with the lower border of the scarf . . . The incision in the neck commenced on the left side, 2½ inches below the angle of the jaw and almost in a direct line with it, nearly severing the vessels on that side, cutting the windpipe completely in two and terminating on the opposite side 1½ inches below the angle of the right jaw . . . The blood was running down the gutter into the drain in the opposite direction from the feet. There was about 1lb of clotted blood close by the body . . .

The body was taken to St George's mortuary in Cable Street and identification was not certain. The hysterical Mary Malcolm, a tailor's wife from Eagle Street, believed she had received a 'death visitant' (i.e. a ghost appearing at the moment of its host's death) of her sister, Elizabeth Watts. In the mortuary, Mrs Malcolm identified the murdered woman by an adder bite on her leg. She was still persisting with this story when the inquest was held and the apparently deceased Elizabeth Watts (by now Mrs Stokes) turned up! It was left to Constable Walter Stride, Liz's nephew by marriage, to make the definitive identification, but he seems to have gone by the mortuary photograph, not the corpse itself.

Bagster Phillips also visited Dutfield's Yard and he carried out the post mortem the following afternoon with Blackwell:

> There was a clean-cut incision on the neck. It was 6 in. in length and commenced 2½ in. in a straight line below the angle of the jaw, ½in. over an undivided muscle and then becoming deeper, dividing the sheath. The cut was very clean and deviated a little downwards. The artery and other vessels in the sheath were all cut through . . . From this it was evident that the haemorrhage was caused through the partial severance of the left carotid.

At the inquest of October 5, Phillips's opinions of the murderer's attack differed from Blackwell's:

> . . . the deceased was seized by the shoulders, pressed to the ground, and the perpetrator of the deed was on the left side when he inflicted the wound. The cut was made from left to right of the deceased . . . The knife was not sharp pointed, but round and an inch across . . . The injuries would only take a few seconds to inflict; it might have been done in two seconds . . . The deceased was lying on the ground when the wound was inflicted.

Considerable confusion has arisen over Phillips's views on the murder of Elizabeth Stride. The dead woman had mud (it was a wet night) on her left side and head. This would fit if her killer pushed her down on that side. But if (as Phillips says) he began his attack on the deceased's left, then he would have had to have yanked her head round to an almost impossible angle and he must have been on her right to do it.

An undertaker named Hawkes, of Banner Street, moved by the ultimate tragedy in Elizabeth Stride's life, arranged and paid for the funeral, in pauper's grave Number 15509 in the East London Cemetery.

At the time, virtually everyone assumed that Liz Stride was another Ripper victim, but virtually everyone also added Emma Smith and Martha Tabram to the list and, even as late as 1891, Frances Coles (Carrotty Nell). More careful modern analysis, away from the rising tide of panic in the Abyss, points out the obvious differences. Liz was killed with a short, round-ended knife, unlike the pointed weapon of the other murders. There was no sign of punching or manual strangulation. The body was found on its side, not on its back as in all other cases and, most obviously of all, there were no bodily mutilations. There seems little doubt that the scene witnessed by Israel Schwartz, of 22 Ellen Street, actually took place. He made a deposition to the police on September 30:

> . . . having got as far as the gateway where the murder was committed, he saw a man stop and speak to a woman, who was standing in the gateway [of Dutfield's Yard]. The man tried to pull the woman into the street, but he turned her round and threw her down on the footway and the woman screamed three times, but not very loudly.

It was at this point that Schwartz crossed the road and noticed a second man lighting his pipe. The woman's assailant shouted out 'Lipski' and the man with the pipe began to approach Schwartz who ran the length of Berner Street in the direction of the railway arch. It is of course possible that Liz Stride's assailant left her and in the next fifteen minutes, she met Jack at the same spot. Equally likely is that the fight between Liz and her client carried on after Schwartz's exit and resulted in her death inside Dutfield's Yard.

All we can do is to leave a question mark hanging over Pauper Grave Number 15509.

Twelve minutes walk from Berner Street lies Mitre Square. Unaware of the finding of Liz Stride's body three quarters of an hour earlier, Constable Edward Watkins of the City of London Force clattered into the Square in his hobnailed boots. His beat covered Duke Street, Creechurch Lane, Leadenhall Street, Mitre Square and St James's Place. He had last entered the Square itself fourteen or fifteen minutes earlier and it had been empty. Now there was a woman's body lying on the pavement at the southwest corner, outside an empty house. He ran to the warehouses of Kearley and Tonge across the Square and found George Morris, the nightwatchman, crying, 'For God's sake, mate, come to assist me. There's another woman cut up to pieces.'

On that mild, damp night, Morris had had the warehouse door open, yet he had heard nothing until Watkins arrived at the double. He dashed into Aldgate behind the Square and found City Constable 964 James Harvey on patrol. Harvey had passed the end of Church Passage (in direct line with the body) five minutes earlier and had heard and seen nothing. City Constable 814 Holland joined him as they ran back to Mitre Square, but he veered off to rouse Dr George Sequeira whose surgery was in Jewry Street. Within twenty minutes the Square was full of policemen - Inspector Edward Collard from Bishopsgate police station around the corner, Inspector James McWilliam, Head of

The fourth Ripper site and the second on the single night of the 'double event'. This was Mitre Square in the 1920s. None of the original buildings is standing now.

The official police map of Mitre Square with Kate Eddowes' body in situ. With a heavy irony, the house 'occupied by Police Constable' is shown on the left.

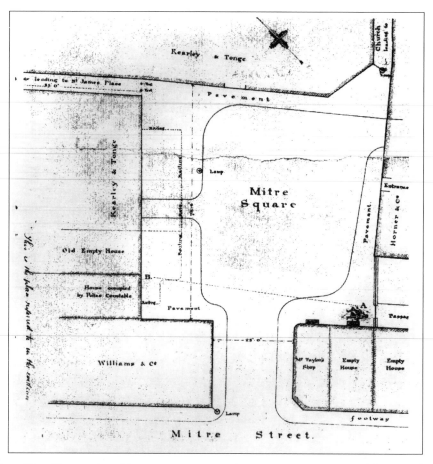

the City Detective Department, and numerous constables. Police Surgeon Frederick Brown joined them, as did, eventually, the highest ranking policeman to visit any of the Ripper sites so far, Major Henry Smith, Acting Commissioner of the City Force. Had the body been found a few feet away, the matter would have been in the jurisdiction of the Metropolitan Force, like all the other Ripper killings. The press at the time had little but contempt for the Met and trumpeted the arrival of the City men as a great breakthrough. In fact McWilliam's report was so useless that Henry Matthews, the Home Secretary, concluded 'They evidently want to tell us nothing.'

Dr Brown's description, both *in situ* and on the mortuary slab in Golden Lane, is the fullest we have of any Ripper victim.

> The body was on its back, the head turned to the left shoulder. The arms by the side of the body as if they had fallen there. Both palms upwards, the fingers slightly bent . . . Left leg extended in a line with the body. The abdomen was exposed. Right leg bent at the thigh and knee. The throat cut across. The intestines were drawn out to a large extent and placed over the right shoulder -

they were smeared over with some feculent matter. A piece of about two feet was quite detached from the body and placed between the body and left arm, apparently by design. The lobe and auricle of the right ear was cut obliquely through . . .

Body was quite warm. No death stiffening had taken place. She must have been dead most likely within the half hour. No blood on the skin of the abdomen or secretion of any kind on the thighs . . . There was no sign of recent connection.

On the Sunday afternoon, Brown carried out the post-mortem at the Golden Lane mortuary and sketches as well as photographs of the dead woman were made. The whole question of photographic evidence is of course what this book is all about. It has only been within the last eight years that photographs of all five Ripper victims have surfaced. Where they were in the intervening years is anybody's guess. It may be of course that there are other photographs which have either been lost, stolen or strayed; or they may yet turn up, but it seems likely that as the murders increased, the efforts of everybody - police, surgeons, coroners - involved with the case doubled and more care was taken with the tiny details that would hopefully catch Jack. So whereas we only have one photograph of Polly Nichols, Annie Chapman and Liz Stride, we have three of Kate Eddowes and two sketches, one of her face and one of her trunk.

It was the condition of the face that marked a new twist in the Ripper killings.

There was a cut [reported Brown] about a quarter of an inch through the lower left eyelid, dividing the structures completely through. The upper eyelid on that side, there was a scratch through the skin on the left upper eyelid, near to the angle of the nose. The right eyelid was cut through to about half an inch.

There was a deep cut over the bridge of the nose, extending from the left border of the nasal bone down near to the angle of the jaw on the right side of the cheek. This cut went into the bone and divided all the structures of the cheek except the mucous membrane of the mouth. The tip of the nose was quite detached . . . About half an inch from the top of the nose was another oblique cut. There was a cut on the right angle of the mouth as if the cut of a point of a knife . . . There was on each side of the cheek a cut which peeled up the skin, forming a triangular flap about an inch and a half.

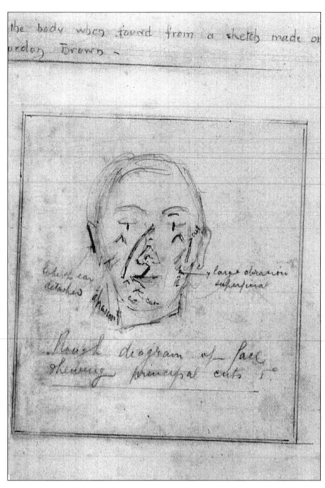

The sketch made of the mutilations to Kate Eddowes' face. The triangular cuts on the cheeks have led some Ripperologists to conjecture a Masonic connection.

The throat wounds were very similar to those of Annie Chapman and the actual cause of death was haemorrhage from the left carotid artery. Death, Brown believed, would have been 'immediate'. Let us hope so.

Space precludes listing all the injuries to Kate Eddowes, but the mutilations were appalling and the worst yet. She had been ripped upwards from the pubis to the breast bone. Her liver had been stabbed and slit with a very sharp instrument. A similar stab had been made in the left groin and the labia were separated. The intestines had been detached and about two feet of the colon had been cut away. Although the vagina and cervix were uninjured, 'the rest of the womb had been taken away with some of the ligaments' and the 'left kidney carefully taken out and removed.'

At the inquest, Brown offered his views about the murderer's methods. He believed that the killer must have 'a great deal' of medical knowledge, but inclined to the view that he was used to working on animal dissection rather than operating on humans. The actual death would be accomplished very quickly, without noise or struggle and the wounds were such that the murderer would have very little blood on him. The mutilations would have taken about five minutes, were the act of one person and the slicing of the face was presumably intended to disfigure the corpse.

The police had compiled a very detailed list of the dead woman's clothes and belongings in order to identify her. She wore a black straw bonnet, cloth jacket, chintz skirt over two others, a linsey bodice, petticoat, chemise and a pair of men's lace up boots. She wore no drawers or stays (not unusual among the Victorian poor and certainly not among prostitutes). She carried a number of handkerchiefs, pieces of rag, clay pipes, a tin box of tea, sugar, a flannel and six pieces of soap, a comb, a ball of hemp, a pair of specs, a spoon and a knife and an apron so dirty that the white cloth appeared black. The rest of this apron provided a possible clue and will be discussed in the next chapter.

On the dead woman's left forearm were the initials 'T.C.', but it was the pawn tickets found in her mustard tin that led to her identification. One was in the name of Emily Birrell or Burrell of 52 White's Row, who turned out to be a drinking buddy of the dead woman. The other was for Jane Kelly, an alias often used by Kate Eddowes after 1881 when she lived on and off with market porter John Kelly, who came forward and identified his common law wife on reading about the tickets in the papers. The 'T.C.' on Kate's arm were the initials of Tom Conway, her common law husband before Kelly.

Kate Eddowes was buried on October 8 in the London Cemetery where her scarlet sisters lay. This time Hawkes again bore the expense, but this time it wasn't possible to evade the crowds and they lined the streets in silent token of respect and of a mark of their own terror.

Thomas Bowyer was known as 'Indian Harry' among the people of the Abyss. An Indian army pensioner, he lived at 37 Dorset Street, a few doors up from Miller's Court at 26. On the morning of Friday November 9, Lord Mayor's Day (when the whole of the East End usually turned out onto the streets in whatever finery it could muster), Bowyer went to call on Mary Jane Kelly to collect the rent she owed to her landlord and his boss, John McCarthy. He knocked on her door at 10.45, having walked the narrow entrance to the Court between McCarthy's chandler's shop and Number 26. Kelly's dingy room was to his right, entered by one door only. There was no reply, so he tried the spring lock. It didn't work. He reached in through a long-broken window pane and pulled aside a coat hanging there by way of a curtain. The sight that met him was the most revolting of all the Ripper murders. Bowyer dashed off to tell McCarthy in his shop at the entrance to the Court. McCarthy took one look at all that was left of Mary Kelly and sent Bowyer for the police.

Inspector Walter Beck was at Commercial Street police station and he and Detective Constable Walter Dew of H Division ran back with him. It was now that senior police politics intervened because there was indecision as to whether bloodhounds were going to be used. The fact that this was the first Ripper killing to take place indoors meant that the likelihood was there would be clues everywhere. No policeman entered Kelly's room until 1.30 p.m., when Superintendent Thomas Arnold, Head of H Division and a man closely connected with other Ripper killings, arrived with orders to break down the door.

The police surgeons summoned to Miller's Court were Thomas Bond, attached to A Division, and the by now inevitable Bagster Phillips. Bond's report was long missing, but was sent to Scotland Yard in 1987:

> The body was lying naked [this is wrong. Mary was still wearing a chemise, much hacked about] in the middle of the bed, the shoulders flat, but the axis of the body inclined to the left . . . The head was turned on the left

The last of the Ripper sites - the narrow, unlit entrance to Miller's Court in Dorset Street.

Mary Kelly's room at 13, Miller's Court. The window right of centre was covered on the inside with a rough curtain.

cheek. The left arm was close to the body and rested on the mattress, the elbow bent and the forearm supine with the fingers clenched. The legs were wide apart, the left thigh at right angles to the trunk and the right forming an obtuse angle with the pubes.

The whole of the surface of the abdomen and thighs was removed and the abdominal cavity emptied of its viscera. The breasts were cut off, the arms mutilated by several jagged wounds and the face hacked beyond recognition of the features. The tissues of the neck were severed all round down to the bone.

The viscera were found in various parts viz; the uterus and kidneys with one breast under the head, the other breast by the right foot, the liver between the feet, the intestines by the right side and the spleen by the left side of the body. The flaps from the abdomen and thighs were on a table.

With difficulty the carrier's cart inched its way through the crowds that had abandoned the Lord Mayor's procession with its gilded carriages and helmeted pikemen of the City's Honourable Artillery Company. The remains of Mary Kelly, with photographs taken from at least two angles in her tiny room, were transferred to Shoreditch mortuary.

There the next day, Bond and Bagster Phillips carried out the post mortem. Bond wrote later that day:

The face was gashed in all directions, the nose, cheeks, eyebrows and ears being partly removed. The lips were blanched and cut by several incisions running obliquely down to the chin. There were also numerous cuts extending irregularly across all the features.

The neck was cut through the skin and other tissues right down to the vertebrae, the 5th and 6th being deeply notched. The skin cuts in the front of the neck showed distinct ecchymosis [indicating bruising made by a slow, deliberate cut]. The air passage was cut at the lower part of the larynx through the cricoid cartilage.

Both breasts were removed by more or less circular incisions, the muscles down to the ribs being attached to the breasts. The intercostals [muscles] between the 4th, 5th and 6th ribs were cut through and the contents of the thorax visible through the openings.

The skin and tissues of the abdomen from the costal

arch to the pubes were removed in three large flaps. The right thigh was denuded in front of the bone, the flap of skin, including the external organs of generation and part of the right buttock. The left thigh was stripped of skin, fascia and muscles as far as the knee.

The left calf showed a long gash though skin and tissues to the deep muscles and reaching from the knee to 5 ins. above the ankle.

Both arms and forearms had extensive and jagged wounds.

The right thumb showed a small superficial incision about 1 in. long, with extravasation of blood in the skin and there were several abrasions on the back of the hand moreover showing the same condition.

On opening the thorax it was found that the right lung was minimally adherent by old firm adhesions. The lower part of the lung was broken and torn away. The left lung was intact: it was adherent at the apex and there were a few adhesions over the side.

The pericardium was open below and the heart absent.

The other surviving photograph from 13 Miller's Court. Mary Kelly's hand can be made out on the extreme left. On the table in the distance is the flesh cut from her body.

Two pieces of information, one false, the other unknown, clouded the analysis of Mary Kelly's death for many years. Because Bond's report was lost and because Bagster Phillips gave almost nothing away at the inquest (so much so that some Ripperologists imply that he was 'nobbled' so that he would not give away some incriminating piece of evidence), speculation arose about the nature of Mary's mutilations. Her breasts were said to be dumped on her side table, her entrails hung from picture rails. And, most touching of all, she was said to have been three months pregnant. All this was the invention of the press. The fact that her heart was missing was not known by Ripperologists until 1987 when Bond's report turned up.

Dr Bond was asked by Dr Robert Anderson, Assistant Commissioner at Scotland Yard and the man in charge of the Ripper investigation from early October, to compile a dossier on the similarities in the Ripper's M.O. Bond's findings are valuable because they were made by an expert on the spot. He believed that all five murders were committed by the same hand (there is today some doubt about Liz Stride) and that in the first four cases, the throats were cut from left to right. There was a great deal of speculation at the time and has been since as to whether the Ripper was right- or left-handed or both. The answer to that question depends on the nature of the wounds themselves. If the Ripper slashed their throats as he hurried past them, then the wounds might be on the left side of the victim if their killer were right-handed. If he made his cuts deliberately, however (and the depth of the cuts would indicate this to be more likely), while kneeling astride his victim (perhaps already semiconscious because of strangulation), then it is more likely the killer was left-handed, applying the point of the knife backhand. Only ten percent of people today are left-handed and this figure would probably have been lower in Victorian England, especially among the educated classes, who would have been forced to use their right hand when being taught to write.

Bond quite rightly deduced that all five women had their throats cut and were lain down before the mutilations began.

The timing of the murders was difficult. No clinical thermometer seems to have been used to check the body's temperature per rectum. The various doctors working on the case felt the hands, face and throat and Bond noticed that Mary Kelly's body was stiffening with rigor mortis as he examined her at Miller's Court at about 2 o'clock in the afternoon of November 9. Rigor mortis, lividity and decomposition of bodies varies depending on the temperature, both internal and external, the conditions (whether dry or damp) and therefore the time of day or even the season of the year. It is not likely that any of the Ripper death timings was that accurate, but the passing of patrolling policemen in Mitre Square and the arrival of Louis Diemschütz at Dutfield's Yard give us reasonable reliability in the cases of Kate Eddowes and Liz Stride.

Bond believed that all five attacks had been so sudden that no victim was able to cry out or fight back before they died. No debris was found under the dead women's nails because none was looked for. Corny though this ploy is - the telltale scratches on a killer's cheek has hanged many a fictional murderer - most women fighting for their lives would have used nails, teeth, boots, *anything* to stay alive. There have been attempts to suggest that at least one of the Ripper's victims was drugged (perhaps with poisoned grapes) to make her comatose, but the evidence is flimsy. If a powerful man punched his victim several times in the jaw (the bruising on three of the victims indicates this) or gripped their throats so hard that they passed out quickly (bruising also supports this) then little or no noise would have been made. The cry of 'Oh, murder!' that was heard from Mary Kelly's room in the early hours of November 9 may be the exception to Bond's rule, but there is no evidence that it came from the lips of Mary Kelly.

According to Bond, the Ripper struck in the first four cases from the victim's right side. There was plenty of room in the open air, even in the relatively restricted spaces at the back of 29 Hanbury Street and in Dutfield's Yard for this to be the case. Again, Mary Kelly is different. The bed in her room was pushed into the corner, so that her killer would have had to have worked from above her as she lay on the bed or from her left in the centre of the room.

The layman's view of knife killers is that they must be saturated with blood when they leave the murder scene. Bond pointed out that this was not necessarily so. Certainly the Ripper's arms and hands would be bloody and his clothes smeared, but there were ways of disguising this, even conceivably when walking past patrolling policemen. J.H.H. Gauté and Robin Odell, the authors of *Murder What Dunnit* (they claim that 'The Grand Master of the knife murder was Jack the Ripper'), make the point that the shape of blood splashes, on the body, on furniture, on walls near the body, all tell their own story. As long as the Ripper was out of the way of the carotid artery when he sliced through it, then he would not be covered in blood. The fact remains of course that the Abyss was full of slaughterhouses of the type that Canon Samuel Barnett wanted removed because of their brutalizing effect on the locals. Men wearing bloody overalls and aprons were a commonplace in the area and this fact alone led to the arrest and near-lynching of one suspect.

Bond described the murder weapon (which was never found) as being a strong-bladed knife, at least six inches long, very sharp and with a point. It could have been a clasp knife, or the sort carried by a butcher or surgeon.

Two of Bond's deductions deal with the psychology of the murderer and are a fascinating insight into the attempt of somewhat bewildered science to grapple with the new phenomenon of the serial killer. We shall look at them in the final chapter. The most contentious claim made by Bond, with which all other doctors on the case disagreed, was his eighth point:

> In each case the mutilation was inflicted by a person who had no scientific nor anatomical knowledge. In my opinion he does not even possess the technical knowledge of a butcher or horse slaughterer or any person accustomed to cut up dead animals.

Arguments still rage over this. Whether Jack was working in the estimated two hours it took to mutilate Mary Kelly with the help of the firelight in her room, or the five minutes or so he took to disembowel Kate Eddowes in the near-blackness of Mitre Square, his ability to cut out uteri, a heart and a kidney surely gives the lie to Bond's assertions. There may be an element of professional pique in the good doctor's remarks. Whoever he was, the Whitechapel murderer was deranged. Surgeons like Bond were not deranged people. No one with a medical skill could be.

Therefore, Jack was not a surgeon. Later Ripperologists have disagreed. The 'Mad Doctor' theory runs like a thread of surgical suture throughout the Ripper case and the finger has been pointed at more doctors than anyone else.

Mary Jane Kelly was buried at the expense of Henry Wilton, the verger of St Leonard's Church, Shoreditch on Monday November 19. This time the crowd could be numbered in thousands. Women wept, murmuring 'God forgive her!'

No doubt He already had.

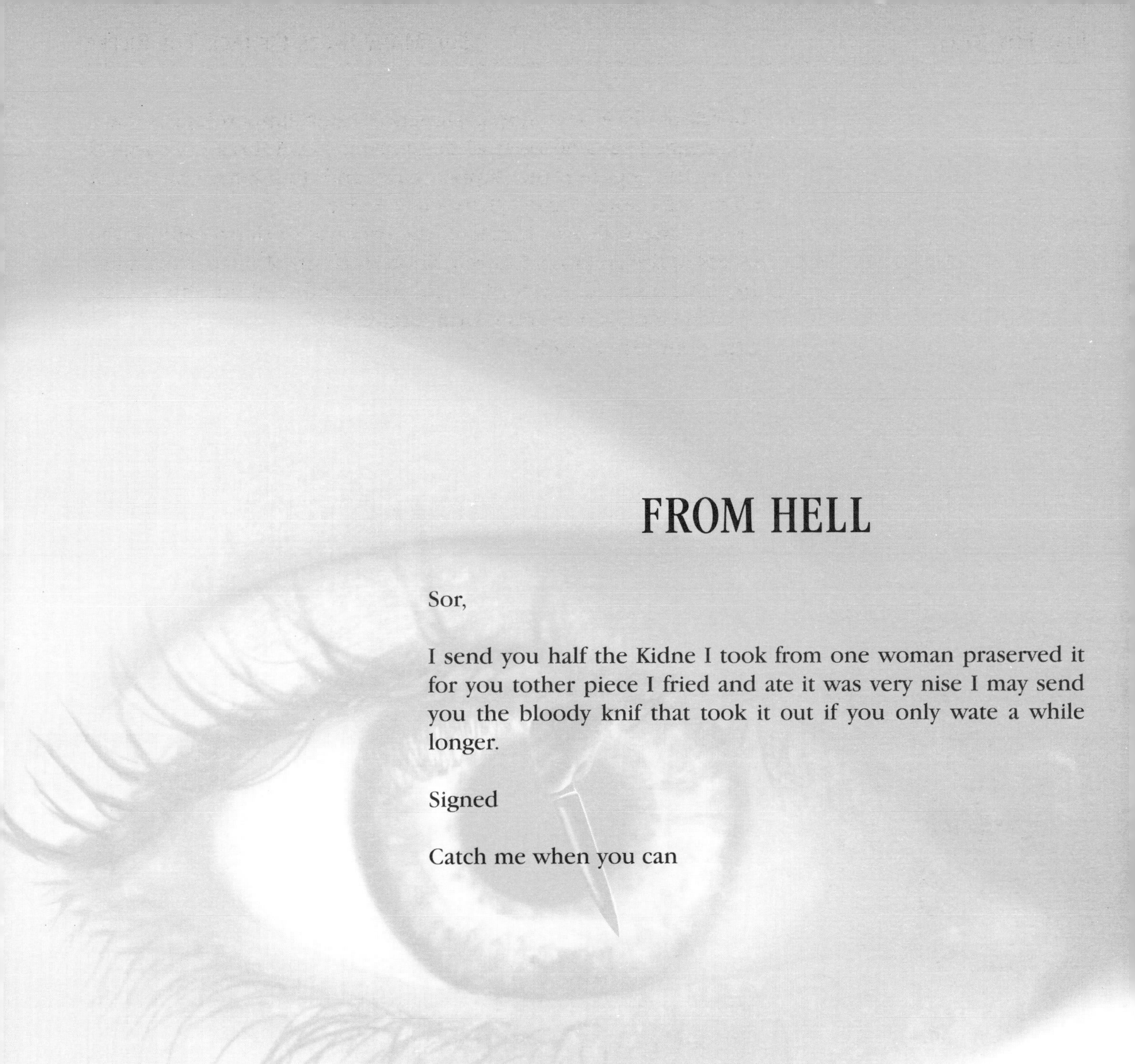

FROM HELL

Sor,

I send you half the Kidne I took from one woman praserved it for you tother piece I fried and ate it was very nise I may send you the bloody knif that took it out if you only wate a while longer.

Signed

Catch me when you can

Today, the most important evidence of a killing comes from the murder site itself. Scene of crime officers, photographers, police surgeons, pathologists, fingerprint experts and dozens more all play their part in attempting to reconstruct the last hours, minutes and seconds of a person's life. We have seen already how limited all this was in 1888.

Violence was common enough in the Abyss - all its middle class visitors comment on it and were shocked by it. Mary Kelly's supposed cry of 'Oh, murder' in the early hours of November 9 was heard independently by three people, yet such cries were so common that no one stirred to investigate. But violence of this type - near identical attacks on five women of the same class in the space of ten weeks and all within a mile radius - was utterly unknown and the police chased their own tails in an attempt to drag every ounce of information from every clue they could find.

THE EYEWITNESSES

It is now realized that the average human makes an appalling eyewitness. If six people are sitting in a room and a gunman bursts in, kills one of them and rushes out, the police will probably be given five totally different descriptions of the killer. Since no one seems to have caught Jack the Ripper in the act, the element of traumatizing shock is removed from the eyewitness accounts. Even so, we are relying on people's memories, days and sometimes weeks after the event, of shadowy figures glimpsed briefly in poor light. Few men seen in the company of the low life whores of the Abyss would want to be seen and some at least appear to have gone to some lengths to keep their faces hidden, not because they were Jack the Ripper (although one of them probably was on two occasions) but because they were importuning in the street.

No one seems to have been seen with Polly Nichols in Buck's Row, but nightwatchman Patrick Mulshaw, who guarded a sewage works in parallel Winthrop Street, was informed of the murder by an unknown man between three and four in the morning of August 31. 'Watchman, old man, I believe somebody is murdered down the street.' This man could of course have been one of hundreds of innocent passers-by on his way to work that morning, but equally, a guilty man with the mind of a psychopath might well have felt compelled to say something about the awful crime he had just committed when confronted with a nosey member of the public at that moment, especially if that crime was his first.

Annie Chapman's last moments were rather more public and it is noticeable that as the killings increased, everyone became more aware, more on edge. Police patrols were stepped up, vigilante committees were formed, eyes were everywhere. Perhaps this is why the Ripper killed Mary Kelly indoors - the streets were too hot for him by November 9. Elizabeth Durrell, also known as Elizabeth Long, identified Annie Chapman in the mortuary. At her inquest she said she had seen her talking to a man, whom she only saw from behind, along Hanbury Street at about five in the morning. The timing here is crucial, because Annie was the only one of the five to die in the daylight. If Mrs Durrell is right, the man she saw is very likely to have been the Ripper. He was of shabby genteel appearance, with a dark complexion, looking rather 'foreign' (Jewish). He wore a deerstalker cap and a dark coat and was a little taller than Annie (who was about 5 ft 1 inch). The immediate problem with eyewitness accounts is that we need to know more than we do about the witness. The fact that Mrs Durrell used two names does not necessarily make her suspect (though I would bet a defending barrister would have crucified people like her had the Ripper case ever come to court) and we have no idea of her views on the Jews, whose recent influx was destroying the Irish-cockney community of the Abyss. Certainly, there was to be a wave of anti-Semitism over the Ripper killings with the arrest of 'Leather Apron' on September 10.

Another man was seen with a prostitute entering 29 Hanbury Street at about 2 o'clock on the morning of September 8. He too was dark and swarthy, but his clothes do not match those of the man seen by Mrs Durrell. His jacket was short, as were his waistcoat and trousers and he wore a black scarf and black felt hat. He was about thirty-seven years old and had a beard and moustache. This description, including his foreign accent, was given to a reporter from the *Star* newspaper. The informant was probably a prostitute, Emily Walter, who said she was accosted for business by a similar man. The passage alongside Number 29 Hanbury Street was ideal for the quick rough sex offered by the ladies of the Whitechapel Night - it was dark and quiet and narrow enough to use the walls for support. Again, a prostitute like Emily Walter does not make a good witness. She did not testify at Annie Chapman's inquest and we are left to wonder how the *Star*'s reporter found her, whether any money changed hands and how leading were his questions. In any case, if Mrs Durrell's sighting is correct, the man Emily Walter saw is unlikely to have been the Ripper - unless he had sex with Annie at two o'clock, went home to change and met her again three hours later at the same place!

Today, a policeman's eyewitness testimony would be taken very seriously because the police are trained to be observant and to remain calm in crisis situations. As we shall see in the next chapter, the police of the Ripper's day were pale reflections of their modern counterparts and the evidence of Constable 452H William Smith would be almost totally unhelpful were it not for the fact that the description is so similar to others. He was on duty on the night of Liz Stride's murder and his beat took him, at the time-honoured pace of 2½ miles an hour, between twenty-five and thirty minutes. At about half past twelve he saw Liz (whose body he subsequently saw surrounded by onlookers) in the rain opposite Dutfield's Yard. Smith's man was cleanshaven (ruling out Emily Walter's character), about twenty-eight years old, 5ft 7in tall, wearing dark clothes and a dark felt deerstalker hat. Most ominously, he was carrying a parcel, about 18 inches long and 6-8 inches wide, wrapped in newspaper. The timing is quite good. We know that Liz Stride died between 12.45 and 1 p.m. because of the arrival of Louis Diemschütz. Even so, the ostentatious package is almost too good to be true.

Israel Schwartz was in the same street and may have seen the same man. He gave a description to the police and a slightly different one to the *Star*. This may be a trick of memory, but it is more likely a problem of semantics and again it makes Schwartz an unreliable witness. He had only recently arrived in England from Hungary and he seems to have spoken little or no English. The police and presumably the *Star* would have used interpreters and in the very precise science of identification, this raises all sorts of problems. Schwartz is also unreliable because he was afraid. It was he who saw a woman who was probably Liz Stride thrown to the ground and he immediately crossed the street; the phenomenon of standing idly by, so deplored in the 1990s is not, clearly, new. He told the *Star* that the assailant was half-drunk. Schwartz then caught sight of a second man, lighting his pipe, having just come out of a nearby pub and heard the woman's assailant shout 'Lipski' (which may have been a warning or simply an expletive at recognizing Schwartz's obviously Jewish appearance). Either way, Schwartz felt threatened and ran.

Despite the obvious shakiness of Schwartz's senses at the time, he gave police descriptions of both men. The first (i.e. Liz's assailant) was about thirty years old, 5ft 5in tall with a fair complexion, a small brown moustache, a full face, broad shoulders, a dark jacket and trousers, with a black peaked cap. Unlike the man seen by Constable Smith, he carried nothing in his hands. The second man was thirty-five, much taller at 5ft 11in, with fresh complexion, light brown hair, a dark overcoat and wide-brimmed dark felt hat. He carried a clay pipe. It is probably coincidence, but notice that the *Jew's* testimony is of two patently Gentile thugs, whereas the evidence of Emily Walter and Elizabeth

Durrell is clearly of shady Jews. This racial sparring did an increasingly desperate police force no favours at all.

James Brown testified at Liz Stride's inquest. He was a dock labourer from Fairclough Street around the corner from Dutfield's Yard and saw Long Liz leaning against the wall of the Board School. With her was a thickset man, about 5ft 7in tall, with a heel-length coat of the type worn by the Jews (although Brown does not say he was Jewish). He heard Liz Stride say 'No, not tonight. Maybe some other night.' The problem with Brown's testimony is that he made this sighting at 12.45 a.m., in other words simultaneously with Schwartz's violent sighting some yards away at the entrance to Dutfield's Yard. It is likely that Brown misidentified Liz Stride.

The last eyewitness in the Berner Street murder is the least reliable of all, possibly in the whole Ripper case. Matthew Packer was a fifty-eight year old fruiterer who lived over his shop at 44 Berner Street, only two doors down from the entrance to Dutfield's Yard. He had closed his shop at 12.30 a.m., and neither he nor his wife nor his two lodgers had seen or heard anything suspicious when answering door-to-door enquiries made by the police the following day. However, two private detectives, Grand of the Strand (!) and his partner J.H. Batchelor, working on behalf of the *Evening News*, got a different story from him. At 11.45, Packer told the detectives a woman with a white flower pinned to her jacket (other witnesses remembered Liz Stride wearing one on the night she died) came into his shop and her male companion bought half a pound of black grapes. The

The witness who became a pest - grocer Matthew Packer probably saw the Ripper, but his subsequent stories to the press make him an unreliable witness.

man was about 5ft 7in tall, with dark clothes, a wideawake hat and looked like a clerk. Packer noticed them standing across the road from his shop, eating the grapes in the rain.

Grand and Batchelor took Packer to the Golden Lane mortuary and tried to trick him by showing him the body of Kate Eddowes. Packer told them he'd never seen the woman before. On October 4, they took the fruiterer to the mortuary of St George's-in-the-East and Packer recognized Liz Stride - 'I believe she bought some grapes at my shop about 12 o'clock on Saturday.'

Grand and Batchelor were the sort of 'Holmes and Watson' team the real (as opposed to Conan Doyle's fictional) police dread. But in this case, they got results, even finding a grape stem in the rubbish of Dutfield's Yard that the Met had overlooked. They took Packer on his third visit, this time to Scotland Yard, where he was interviewed personally by the Commissioner of Police, Sir Charles Warren. Packer developed his sighting. The man with Liz Stride was between twenty-five and thirty years old, he wore a long, black buttoned-up coat and an [indecipherable] hat. He had rather broad shoulders, and a rough voice, quickly spoken. He wore no gloves and was between 1½ and 3 inches taller than she was ('Long Liz' was 5ft 5in tall). What is noticeable is that Packer's times vary considerably. He told the house-to-house enquiry team nothing about the grape incident. He told Grand and Batchelor that all this happened between 12 and 12.30. He told Warren it was an hour earlier. Throughout October Packer was talking to the papers again, claiming he had seen Liz Stride's companion several times in the area, both before and after her murder.

Modern police forces are used to the Matthew Packer type. They love the frisson of notoriety that being so close to a murder gives them. It was Packer's one - his only - moment of fame. And it seems that the Victorian police were no more fooled by him than their modern counterparts would be. Packer was not called to Elizabeth Stride's inquest.

Joseph Lawende was altogether more reliable. He was a Polish immigrant who seems to have done better in economic terms than most of his countrymen. He was a travelling salesman in cigarettes and gave two business premises from which he worked. Held up by heavy rain on the night of September 29-30, Lawende and his friends Henry Harris and Joseph Levy stayed late at the Imperial Club in Duke's Place. They left shortly after 1.30 a.m. by the Club clock and on their way saw the woman later identified as Kate Eddowes standing with a man in Church Passage leading into Mitre Square. The others paid no attention, but Lawende saw the man reasonably clearly and the police were so impressed by his evidence that they had it suppressed in the inquest which Lawende attended. In the police depositions, however, Lawende described his man as of medium build and looking like a sailor. He wore a loose pepper-and-salt coloured jacket and a matching grey peaked cap. He wore a red neckerchief, was about thirty with a fair complexion and moustache and stood between 5ft 7in and 5ft 9in. At the time of the sighting, Kate Eddowes was resting her hand on his chest and they appeared to be in affable conversation. Did the mood change as Lawende and his friends walked away? Or did Kate Eddowes give this particular partner the brush off and then bump into Jack?

The last eyewitness account is the most intriguing of all. It concerns George Hutchinson, about whom writers on the Ripper have become increasingly uneasy. Hutchinson was an unemployed labourer who had once been a groom and he lived at Victoria Home, Commercial Street, a night refuge for men. His account of seeing Mary Kelly with a man has been discussed earlier, but his description is just a little too detailed to be true. To begin with he was carrying a parcel about 8 inches long in his left hand, dangling by a strap. He pulled his hat down over his eyes as if *very* anxious not to be seen with Kelly.

Hutchinson told the press:

One man who saw the Ripper at very close quarters and for some time was George Hutchinson, seen here in old age. His extraordinarily precise description has fuelled speculation that Hutchinson might have been the Ripper himself.

> The man was about 5ft 6in in height and 34 to 35 years of age, with dark complexion and dark moustache, turned up at the ends. He was wearing a long, dark coat, trimmed with astrakhan, a white collar, with black necktie, in which was affixed a horseshoe pin. He wore a pair of dark spats with light buttons over button boots and displayed from his waistcoat a massive gold chain. His watch chain had a big seal, with a red stone hanging from it. He had a heavy moustache curled up and dark eyes and bushy eyebrows. He had no side whiskers and his chin was clean shaven. He looked like a foreigner . . .
> . . . and carried a pair of brown kid gloves. He walked very softly and Hutchinson believed that he lived in the area and that he had possibly seen him in Petticoat Lane.

What are we to make of Hutchinson's extraordinarily detailed description? And why did he pay so much attention, hanging around Miller's Court for forty-five minutes? He had known Mary Kelly, by his own admission, for three years and it is likely he was a client of hers. Even if he wasn't, he may have been a voyeur, trying to peep through Mary's broken windows. If that was the case, the coat that served as a curtain was all that screened him - and us - from Jack the Ripper at work. He may of course been merely fond of Mary and concerned for her. There was a kind of hysteria in the Abyss by November 9, and Mary Kelly was archetypically a target. What more natural than that a friend should look out for her? It was probably Hutchinson who was the man in the black wideawake hat standing against the lodging-house wall (Crossingham's?) opposite the Miller's Court entrance. The other possibility about Hutchinson's statement is that in the form written above, it was given to the newspapers. Did they pay him for more detail? Is the portrait more the approximation of what a journalist thought a madman would look like? Most sinister of all, was George Hutchinson describing someone he actually knew, but was perhaps afraid to name?

IS HE THE MURDERER?

Jack the Ripper has assumed a legendary and nightmarish reputation because of phrases like Dr Robert Anderson's 'No one ever saw the Whitechapel murderer.' This is untrue. One or perhaps more of the men described above is Jack. Our only problem is that we don't know which one.

THE CLUES

What clues, if any, did the Ripper leave behind? At Buck's Row, he left nothing but Polly Nichols' body. Extensive searches by officers of H and J Division yielded nothing. And the fact that no one saw or heard anything began to build the legend of the murderous will o' the wisp. On September 7 Inspector Joseph Helson of J Division said, 'at present not an atom of evidence can be obtained to connect any person with the crime.' As far as the murder of Polly Nichols goes, it has stayed that way for 108 years.

Jack got more careless - or was it more arrogant? - when he killed Annie Chapman. Albert Cadoche, a carpenter who lodged at Number 27 Hanbury Street, heard a cry of 'No!' (altogether a more plausible word than Mary Kelly's supposed 'Oh, murder!') followed by a thump as though something hit the fence that divided Number 27 from the murder yard. This was at 5.30 a.m. on September 8, so it is highly likely that Cadoche heard Jack at work. He went on his way to work, however, with suspicions unaroused. The yard itself revealed clues that have, like the whole Ripper story, become legendary. The police found tablets wrapped up in paper, and a torn envelope with the crest of the Sussex regiment and an apron, folded and made of leather, soaking wet near a standpipe. Two combs, a piece of muslin cloth, and two farthings, perhaps brightly polished, completed the evidence, but later newspaper reports mentioned finger rings.

For years, these items, which were no more than the 'valuables' carried by Annie on the last night of her life, assumed gigantic proportions. The coins and rings were said to have been laid out neatly between the dead woman's feet and this was utilized by Ripperologist Stephen Knight to claim that the killing had a ritual Masonic significance. We know that Annie took the tablets and the torn envelope from Crossingham's lodging house. The woman was ill and had recently taken a beating. The rings, plain brass ones that Annie was known to wear, were never found. It is possible that they were ripped from her fingers by her killer in an attempt to make the motive (rather improbably) look like one of theft; it is also possible that the mortuary attendants who stripped the body helped themselves. In the Abyss, everything had a street value.

The leather apron caused a sensation. Police were already looking for a man with that nickname in connection with Polly Nichols' death and here was his stock in trade, only feet from Annie Chapman's body. In fact, the apron belonged to John Richardson whose mother Amelia rented the first two floors of Number 29 Hanbury Street. Richardson had called at the house on his way to work (at his mother's packing case business or as a porter in Spitalfields Market) on September 8 and had sat on the steps beside which Annie's body would be dumped forty five minutes later. He trimmed his boot with an old knife (which was subsequently checked and 'exhonerated' by the police). Whether he left the apron in the yard then or on an earlier occasion is unclear. In any case it carried no signs of bloodstains and was in fact an irritating red herring.

Inevitably, there were few clues left at Berner Street because it is likely that the killer (whether he was Jack or not) was interrupted by Louis Diemschütz. Although the private detectives Grand and Batchelor claim to have found a grape stem in Dutfield's Yard which fitted Matthew Packer's tale, there were no grapes found inside Liz's stomach at the post-mortem so its significance diminishes considerably and destroys utterly the drugged grape theory of Stephen Knight. The dead woman still held a packet of cachous (sweets) in her left hand. All this tells us is that she was relaxed and unsuspecting when the Ripper struck. Without the advantage of fingerprint techniques we cannot tell whether the sweets were ever handled by Liz's killer.

It was the second killing of the 'double event' that was to provide the most enigmatic clues of all. All the items found in Mitre Square near Kate Eddowes' body were proved to belong to the dead woman, but five minutes walk away, in the doorway of Wentworth Model Dwellings in Goulston Street, Constable 254A Alfred Long found the other half of her filthy, torn apron. It was established as Kate's because of a running repair stitched into both pieces. It was covered in blood and 'faecal matter' and had been washed, presumably at a standpipe. The most likely explanation is that the Ripper got out of Mitre Square between police patrols, carrying with him a kidney and a uterus wrapped in the half apron. At Goulston Street, he either abandoned his grisly trophies somewhere where they were never found or transferred them to a different container, dropping the now useless apron as he went.

It was what Long saw above the apron, however, that has caused nearly as much ink to be used as upon the Ripper letters, which began to reach the headlines as the activities of the Autumn of

Writing of a different kind is today all over the walls of Goulston Street where the famous graffiti was found in the Autumn of Terror.

The entrance to Wentworth Buildings in Goulston Street shortly before demolition in the 1970s. On the wall facing us were scrawled the chalk words - 'The Jews Are Not The Men Who Will Be Blamed For Nothing'.

Terror intensified. Written in chalk on the blank brickwork of the doorway entrance to 109 Wentworth Buildings were the words:

The Juwes
Are Not The Men Who Will Be Blamed
For Nothing

There is a great deal of controversy over what Ripperologists call 'The Goulston Street grafitto'. We aren't even sure of the order of the words, still less the capital letters or the exact placing of the words on the wall (all of which might have some significance). Superintendent Thomas Arnold of H Division suggested almost as soon as he became aware of it that the words be erased for fear of a backlash against the Jews. The 'Leather Apron' scare was still very much in the wind and the police feared what today we would call race riots if any more fingers were pointed in the direction of the Chosen People. Sir Charles Warren, the Commissioner of the Met, arrived to find Wentworth Model Dwellings the centre of a great deal of police activity. He agreed with Arnold:

if the writing had been left there would have been an onslaught upon the Jews, property would have been wrecked and lives would probably been lost.

Warren had presided (badly) over the battle in Trafalgar Square on 'Bloody Sunday' the previous year. Unpopular and autocratic, he didn't need another nail in his coffin.

Other policemen of all ranks and in both forces disagreed with his decision. Major Smith of the City Police wrote years later that it was a 'fatal mistake' and 'an unpardonable blunder'. Stephen Knight was to capitalize on the odd spelling of Jews for his Masonic murders theory in 1976 and Ripperologists of three generations have argued over the exact meaning of the double negative. The fact is that there is no definite link between the Goulston Street writing and the Ripper at all. The line may simply have been an anti-Semitic outburst in exasperation of the way the Jews were arriving in vast numbers and taking over the area's economy. Even if it was connected with Kate Eddowes' murder and even if it was written by Jack himself, it would have been almost impossible to have matched the handwriting with that of a suspect. Writing with ink on paper is one thing, but using chalk on a rough surface of bricks in the dark is not likely to produce much of a facsimile.

It is the position of the apron that furnishes the best clue. There can be little doubt that the Ripper dropped it and that he was making his way North East, back into Whitechapel and Spitalfields where the Abyss was, by this time, alive to the murder of Liz Stride. Perhaps this meant that he hadn't killed the Berner Street victim after all and must have been panic-stricken to find so much police activity that he hadn't caused. What it also means is that Jack was going home.

13 Miller's Court, which should have provided more clues than any other murder scene, produced almost nothing to point to a particular attacker. Other than the bed in Mary Kelly's tiny room (about 12ft by 15ft) there were two tables and a fireplace. A print of 'The Fisherman's Widow' hung over the fireplace. There had been a fire in the grate, so fierce that it had melted the solder on a kettle's spout (there was of course no proof that that conflagration had taken place on the night of Mary's murder). Inspector Abberline of H Division stirred the fire's ashy contents and came up with the remains of a jacket, skirt and hat. Other than that they were items of female clothing, nothing else could be established. They were probably Mary's and the fire was probably used to provide light as the only other method was the half candle Abberline found in the room.

There would be no more clues from Jack.

THE RIPPER LETTERS

The first of the Ripper letters was posted to the Central News Agency on September 27 1888. A postcard followed on October 1. They carried the postmarks London EC and London E respectively. The letter, written to 'Dear Boss' was penned in red ink:

> I keep on hearing the police have caught me but they won't fix me just yet. I have laughed when they look so clever and talk about being on the right track. That joke about Leather Apron gave me the real fits. I am down on whores and I shan't quit ripping them till I do get buckled. Grand work the last job was. I gave the lady no time to squeal. How can they catch me now. I love my work and want to start again. You will soon hear of me with my funny little games. I saved some of the proper red stuff in a ginger beer bottle over the last job to write with but it went thick like glue and I can't use it. Red ink is fit enough I hope ha ha. The next job I do I shall clip the ladys ears off and send to the police officers just for jolly wouldn't you. Keep this letter back till I do a bit

more work, then give it straight out. My knife's so nice and sharp I want to get back to work right away if I get a chance. Good luck, yours truly, Jack the Ripper.

Dont mind me giving the trade name.

Wasnt good enough to post this before I get all the red ink off my hands curse it. No luck yet. They say I'm a doctor now ha ha.

The 'Dear Boss' letter, despite its American opening, was clearly written by an articulate penman. It is 'thin' on punctuation, but all the full stops are in place and there isn't a single spelling error or crossing out. Both Robert Anderson and Melville McNaghten, senior policemen at the Yard, believed that this and subsequent letters were written by journalists, Anderson even going so far as to say he knew who it was. Current research has pointed to either Bullen or Best, freelancers for the *Star*, as the most likely culprits. The phraseology - 'down on whores', 'till I do get buckled', 'just for jolly' - and the macabre obsession with blood, sound like a schoolboy prank and an attempt to sound Cockneyesque. The real giveaway, however, is the fact that the letter was addressed to the Central News Agency rather than to the police or a specific newspaper and the section about keeping back news until later suggests an author who knew all about such things.

Hard on the heels of 'Dear Boss' came the 'Saucy Jacky' postcard. This was by a different hand or the same one disguised, and written in red crayon:

I was not codding dear old Boss when I gave you the tip, you'll hear about Saucy Jackys work tomorrow double event this time number one squealed a bit couldn't finish straight off had not time to get ears for police thanks for keeping last letter back till I got to work again. Jack the Ripper.

The phrases 'Boss', 'squeal' and of course the 'trade' name make it likely that the same person wrote both of these. For years the reference to the double event was taken very seriously because it appeared to have been written before the two murders on the same night were made public. Now we know that some papers carried the information on Sunday September 30 so that an enterprising journalist would have no problem incorporating the phrase into his postcard.

One thing was certain. From September 27 onwards the words 'Whitechapel murderer' were to recede. The most infamous killer in history had found a name.

More sinister than either of the above was the nasty mess posted on October 15 to George Lusk, builder and chairman of the Whitechapel Vigilance Committee, who lived at Mile End. It was a small parcel wrapped in brown paper with a London postmark and contained half a human kidney preserved in wine. Lusk took it, though he believed it to be a hoax, to Dr Thomas Openshaw of the London Hospital. Dr Sedgewick Sanders, the City pathologist, saw it too. Controversy still rages over the provenance of the kidney. It was said by the press to be 'ginny', i.e. showing signs of Bright's disease, and as having once belonged to a forty-five year old female. There was, however, no way of deducing sex or age from such an organ in 1888. Whether this was indeed the kidney cut from Kate Eddowes in Mitre Square or a medical student's sick joke has never been entirely resolved. Around the kidney was wrapped the letter postmarked 'From Hell':

George Lusk, builder and chairman of the Whitechapel Vigilance Committee who may have received Kate Eddowes' kidney through the post.

Mr Lusk,

Sor

I send you half the Kidne I took from one woman praserved it for you tother piece I fried and ate it was very nise I may send you the bloody knif that took it out if you only wate a while longer

Signed

Catch me when you can

Mishter Lusk

So we now have to add stage Irish - 'Sor' and 'Mishter' - to the Ripper confusion. This letter is altogether more illiterate in its style, but surely with the unlikely misspelling of knife, our journalist friend has tipped his hand once more.

Altogether nearly two hundred Ripper letters reached the papers or the police and the consensus today is that none of them is genuine. What they undoubtedly did was to waste a great deal of police time which could more valuably have been spent elsewhere. A similar hoax 'confession' was to do precisely the same thing in the case of the Yorkshire Ripper

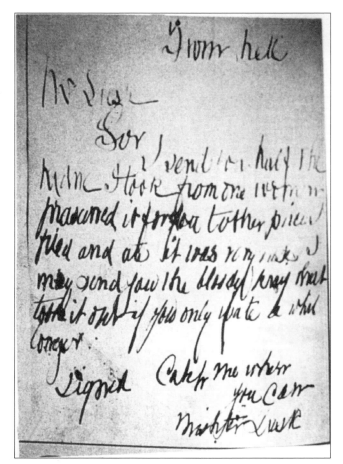

'From Hell' - the illiterate stage-Irish letter wrapped around the kidney sent to George Lusk.

ninety-one years later. Someone sent a tape to George Oldfield, in charge of the investigation into a case which was to claim thirteen lives:

> I'm Jack. I see you are having no luck catching me . . . I reckon your boys are letting you down, George . . . No good looking for fingerprints, you should know by now it's as clean as a whistle. See you soon. 'Bye. Hope you like the catchy tune at the end. Ha-ha.

The technology had changed - the compiler of the tape knew about fingerprints, he knew about the Yorkshire killer's crimes to date and he knew enough about the original Jack to parody his letters quite closely. The tape was broadcast widely, on television, radio and specially setup hot lines. It was delivered in a flat, evil Geordie monotone and so convincing was it that Yorkshireman Peter Sutcliffe, who sounded nothing like the tape, went on to kill three more women before they caught him.

Interestingly, the police caught one Ripper letter hoaxer. She was Maria Coroner, who, for whatever reason, decided to transfer some of the action to her native Bradford. Her letters, sent to a local paper and the Chief Constable of Yorkshire, said that Jack was on his way to Bradford to 'do a little business'. She was charged on October 21 1888 with causing a breach of the peace.

Despite flares of violence from time to time in the East End, with the murders of Rose Mylett in Clark's Yard, Poplar; Alice McKenzie (Clay Pipe Alice) in Castle Alley; Frances Coles (Carrotty Nell) in Swallow Gardens and the discovery of a headless corpse in Pinchin Street over the next three years, the Ripper had already passed into legend and folklore. The people of the Abyss even sang songs about it:

> Ta-ra-ra boom de-ay,
> Ta-ra-ra boom de-ay,
> An East End holiday,
> The Ripper's gone away.

Has he really gone?

Will he ever - really - go?

THE DEFECTIVE FORCE

Walter Dew was a constable at the time of the Ripper killings. He later found fame as the detective who caught Dr Crippen and his accomplice Ethel le Neve for the murder of Belle Elmore (Mrs Crippen).

A Detective's Diary à la Mode

Monday	Papers full of the latest tragedy. One of them suggested that the assassin was a man who wore a blue coat. Arrested three blue coat wearers on suspicion.
Tuesday	The blue coats proved innocent. Released. Evening journal threw out a hint that deed might have been perpetrated by a soldier. Found a small drummer-boy drunk and incapable. Conveyed him to the Station-house.
Wednesday	Drummer-boy released. Letters of anonymous correspondent to daily journal declaring that the outrage could only have been committed by a sailor. Decoyed petty officer of Penny Steamboat on shore and suddenly arrested him.
Thursday	Petty officer allowed to go. Hint thrown out in the Correspondence column that the crime might be traceable to a lunatic. Noticed an old gentleman purchasing a copy of '*Maiwa's Revenge*'. Seized him.
Friday	Lunatic despatched to an asylum. Anonymous letter received, denouncing local clergyman as the criminal. Took the reverend gentleman into custody.
Saturday	Eminent ecclesiastic set at liberty with an apology. Ascertain in a periodical that it is thought just possible the Police may have committed the crime themselves. At the call of duty, finished the week by arresting myself!

Punch, September 22, 1888

Detectives of H Division, Whitechapel, in 1889. The stocky figure in the front row with his head tilted to one side is Sgt William Thick, 'Johnny Upright', with whom Jack London liaised before going down into the Abyss. On his left is Inspector Edmund Reid, actor, singer, conjuror and balloonist as well as damned good copper. In 1876 he became the first man in England to use a parachute, 1000 feet above Luton! His left hand neighbour, Sergeant Eli Caunter, 'Tommy Roundhead', had a very conventional career by comparison.

THE DEFECTIVE FORCE

When Jack London went down into the Abyss in the summer of 1902 he called first on 'Johnny Upright'. He doesn't give us 'Upright's' address nor even his real name, but he was sensible enough to call on a vastly experienced policeman in order to have a bolt-hole to run to if things got too tough on the streets.

'Upright' was in fact Sergeant William Thick who had joined the Metropolitan Police in 1868 and served in B, P and H Divisions. His nickname was explained by his colleague Walter Dew - 'because he was very upright both in his walk and in his methods'. He was 'a holy terror to the local lawbreakers'. He arrested one of the first Ripper suspects, John Pizer, known as 'Leather Apron' and seems to have been heavily involved in the Ripper case from start to finish.

When London met him he had been retired for nine years and was living in Dempsey Street - 'the most respectable street in the East End' as London calls it. He had a wife, two daughters and a 'slavey' or maid of all work. When London arrived, unannounced and in rags, Thick was at church. When they met, London believed their conversation was being overheard by 'an assistant'. The attitude of the whole family changed the next day when London returned suitably dressed and travelling in a hansom cab. Thick found London a safe lodging house a few doors down from his own house.

London's brief insight into Thick's domestic life is tantalizing, because we know so little about the policemen involved in the Ripper case. When Michael Caine played Inspector Abberline of H Division in the Thames-Lorimar mini-series on television, the script writers gave him a drink problem. In my own 'Lestrade' crime fiction series, I have made Abberline a womanizer with a mistress in Penge. Both these interpretations are, I am sure, libellous, but they exist because of the extraordinary secrecy that has always surrounded the Metropolitan Police, which has rather ludicrously been called 'the most public institution in the world.'

The decision made by the Home Secretary and by the Commissioners of the Met and the City forces to explain nothing to the public about the Ripper case was a disastrous one. All it did was to create an atmosphere of suspicion at the time and one of conspiracy ever since.

> In a couple of years (Thick told London), my lease expires. My landlord is one of our kind. He has not put up the rent on any of his houses here and this has enabled us to stay. But any day he may sell, or any day he may die,

which is the same thing as far as we are concerned. The house is bought by a money breeder, who builds a sweat shop on the patch of ground where my grapevine is, adds to the house and rents a room to a family. There you are and Johnny Upright's gone!

Peel's 'Bloody gang' was created in 1829 to cope with a crime wave born of the poverty and distress in the years which followed Waterloo. Robert Peel, the most impressive Home Secretary of the 19th century, was attempting to reduce crime in London and under him he appointed two commissioners (later extended to three) and seventeen divisions, each under the command of a superintendent. The Headquarters of the Metropolitan Police was at Scotland Yard (hopelessly inadequate by the Autumn of Terror in terms of size and facilities) and there were special units like the Horse Patrol and the River Police. By 1888 such specialisation had increased. The docks had their own police, so did the railways and the parks. In many ways, the most innovative change had come in 1843 when the Detective Force was established. Peel had never tackled the police of the square mile City head on. In 1839, they formed their own force, responsible to the Corporation of the City of London. They are still a separate force today.

Although crime was reduced in the capital, it merely spread to the suburbs and by 1856 all counties had by law to set up their own constabularies. Most of them followed the Met pattern of organization. At first, however, the new police were highly unpopular. When the second policeman was killed in the line of duty in 1833, the jury at his murderer's trial called it 'justifiable homicide'.

It is difficult to know what the relationship between the police and the people of the Abyss was by 1888. Nearly sixty years had created an atmosphere of acceptance by the public and there were some surprising links in the Ripper case. Kate Eddowes died within yards of a policeman's house in Mitre Square; Liz Stride was officially identified by her nephew, a constable. One of the apparent suspects, Thomas Cutbush, had an uncle who was a Superintendent at the Yard, in charge of pay and supplies.

Various accounts talk of enormous help being given to the police, especially in their house-to-house enquiries, but I find this difficult to believe. Although the average constable was a working man himself, with dismal pay and unsocial hours, he had defected to the enemy by putting on his blue tunic. Friends of mine who have worked in the East End say that mistrust of the police is universal there. I cannot believe that this is a new situation. Who knows what private resentments and animosities led in 1888 to a witness clamming up? There was intense loyalty among the people of the Abyss to their own - among the Jews of the Ghetto even more so. The question must remain whether the Ripper scare created such waves of panic that this code of silence was broken.

The average copper on the beat patrolled at 2½ miles an hour. He wore a helmet designed to protect his head which by 1888 looked increasingly like that worn by British infantry. The plate was in the form of a starburst and carried the Division letter and personal number of the officer. He wore a dark blue woollen tunic, black hobnailed boots (to which rubber strips were fitted in Whitechapel and Spitalfields to make his approach less obvious) and a cape for bad weather. He carried a bull's eye lantern for night work, a whistle to summon assistance (which had replaced the wooden rattle four years earlier) and an ebony, teak or lignum vitae truncheon fifteen inches long, tucked, since the previous year, into a specially modified pocket in his trousers.

Until the Police Act of 1890 the tradition was to recruit men from the country in the hope that they would be physically tougher than Londoners and untainted by London ways. The slur of bribe-taking has never quite left the Met in fact and bearing in mind the temptations of the 'Whittington syndrome', employing easily-led country bumpkins might be seen as a mistake. Conditions of entry were not demanding. A recruit had to stand 5ft 9in and be able to read and cope with basic arithmetic. Even fifty years later, J.F. Moylan, writing a history of Scotland Yard to commemorate the centenary of the Met, admitted that 'it would be a mistake to suppose that the general standard of entrants is, as yet, other than that of the elementary school.'

BLIND-MAN'S BUFF.

(As played by the Police.)

"TURN ROUND THREE TIMES,
AND CATCH WHOM YOU MAY!"

The satirical magazine Punch *had a field day with the incompetence of the police and seemed to have it in for the Met in particular.*

In that year (1929) over 30 percent of recruits accepted on the grounds of physical fitness and character were rejected on the grounds of insufficient literacy.

The work itself was odd. Much of it was desperately boring, standing at a fixed point (like the constable who refused to leave Spitalfields Market when Henry Holland called him to look at the body of Annie Chapman) or patrolling the same allotted few streets for eight hours. This humdrum routine might suddenly however be shattered by the need to think quickly and act with speed and guts. It was a tall order for below-average men in any period. And faced with the Ripper, many of them were found wanting.

The new copper spent a week or two at Wellington Barracks, learning truncheon or even cutlass drill. He was then posted to his Division and was on the streets, learning as he went, under the tutelage of an older, more experienced hand. When Claude Pain, who would later be involved in the Craig and Bentley case of 1952, joined the Met in 1929, his 'parent' constable showed him how to hook his belt to park railings in order to get some sleep on night duty while appearing to be standing to. Such neglect of duty was not confined to the 1920s. It was tradition, an art. How many boys in blue missed Jack the Ripper because they were dozing somewhere, accepting an affable cuppa from a coffee-stall holder or skipping that particular street just to alleviate the routine?

Some believed they'd missed him and worried about it. Constable Ernest Thompson was on his first night duty on February 13 1891 when he saw the body of Frances Coles (Carrotty Nell) lying dead in Swallow Gardens, Whitechapel. He saw her murderer too, but, in accordance with police orders, stayed with the body and did not give chase. All his life he believed he'd let the Ripper go. Thompson was stabbed to death while making an arrest in November 1900.

Drunkenness was also a problem among the junior ranks of the police. Moylan spoke with pride in 1929 that:

> fifty years ago, when the force was less than half its present size, there were as many defaulters in two or three months as there are now in a year; between three and four hundred men had to be got rid of every year and about the same number had to be reduced in rank and class, mostly for reputed drunkenness.

This does not say much for the quality of officers on the beat in the 1880s.

Among the constables involved in the Ripper case, James Harvey

of the City Force, who gave evidence at Kate Eddowes' inquest, was dismissed in July 1889, reason unknown; Richard Pearse, of the same force, though admittedly off duty, slept through the entire butchery of Kate just yards away from his front door in Mitre Square; Robert Spicer of H Division of the Met was dismissed in April 1889 for being drunk on duty and 'unnecessarily interfering with two private persons'. (Spicer was one of those irritating policemen - mostly from senior ranks - who in later years claimed to have known the identity of the Ripper all along. He saw him accosting women at Liverpool Street Station and would call out cheerily 'Hello, Jack! Still after them?')

Of course there were good policemen on the streets in 1888, men with talent and intelligence, but equally, they were few and far between and most of them were promoted, often into the detective branch, as a result.

Criticism of the police, especially of the Met, came thick and fast from all quarters, especially the press. Some commentators have attributed this to the Met's mishandling of the riots in Trafalgar Square on 'Bloody Sunday', November 13 1887, but this doesn't really hold water. The Grenadier Guards and the Household Cavalry were also involved and came in for no such opprobrium. And the papers which attacked the Met were by no means confined to the radical or gutter press.

To many people, this was the state of affairs in the Autumn of Terror. Jack was able to kill and run at will, while the police were looking in the other direction.

HORRIBLE LONDON; OR, THE PANDEMONIUM OF POSTERS.

'Horrible London' according to Punch *was revelling in the blood of the Ripper crimes. In fact, posters like this were merely the 1880s version of the Newgate ballads of the 18th century and the video nasties of today.*

What was done, as a result of increasing pressure and increasing hysteria? Numbers of constables were drafted in from other Divisions, though as Commissioner Sir Charles Warren pointed out, all that did was to denude other areas of the Metropolis. Private individuals, like the builder and music hall restorer George Lusk, formed their own local Vigilance Committees (today's Neighbourhood Watch, only for real!) and private detectives like Batchelor and Grand were hired. The Area of Search for house-to-house enquiries was increased, but incredibly excluded Buck's Row and Berner Street where two of the murders had been committed. Eighty thousand handbills were stuck up on greasy walls and grimy windows - 'Ghastly Murder' appeared everywhere. In a fascinating precursor of today's obsession with violence and political correctness, *Punch,* on October 13, attacked the handbill stickers for actually encouraging violence in 'The Pandemonium of the Posters':

> There were men
>
> At murderous work in malodorous den.
>
> And ghoul-women gruesomely staring.
>
> The whole sordid drama of murder and guilt,
>
> The steel that strikes home and the blood that is spilt.

But in any case, all the actions of the men on the beat were dictated, as they still are, from the men above. *Punch* referred to the plain clothes men of the CID as 'The Defective Force', but as we shall see, their hands were effectively tied by appalling ineptness from higher still.

The Criminal Investigation Department had replaced the earlier Detective Branch only ten years before the Ripper struck and was born in humiliation and corruption. At the famous 'trial of the detectives' in 1877 a number of Scotland Yard men had been found guilty of bribe-taking and fraud. They were dismissed, but the stench covered everyone. A young lawyer named Howard Vincent, in a move impossible today, suggested to the then Home Secretary that a Criminal Investigation Department be set up with himself at its head. In an equally amateurish nightmare, the government accepted and the CID was born. It is difficult, because of missing files and the appallingly cavalier work of file-keepers of the last century, to be absolutely accurate about who ran the Ripper case on the ground. I think the most important detectives in the Autumn of Terror were Chief Inspector Swanson, Superintendent Arnold and Inspector Abberline.

Frederick George Abberline is the best known name among the Ripper hunters. No photograph of him has survived. In Met records he is described as 5ft 9½in tall, with a fresh complexion, hazel eyes and brown hair. His huge Piccadilly Weepers (sidewhiskers) were rather old-fashioned by 1888 and junior coppers like Walter Dew thought he looked and spoke like a bank manager. He joined the Met, from a position as clocksmith in Dorset in 1863 and became an Inspector ten years later, attached to H Division in Whitechapel. In 1878, when Vincent organized the CID, Abberline was head of the Department in his Division. He was a First Class Inspector by 1888 and actually working out of Headquarters at Scotland Yard, but his intimate knowledge of the killing grounds made him indispensable. We know little of Abberline other than from a book of press cuttings he compiled later in life. According to that, he had received no less than eighty-four citations. Everyone who writes of Abberline, however, whether above or below him on the Met ladder, agrees on his ability, dedication and efficiency.

In the centenary year of the killings, the Evening Standard referred to Abberline's diaries, three leatherbound volumes supposedly written between 1892 and 1915 and full of cryptic 'clues' which do not ring true from the pen of a down-to-earth, logical policeman. The diaries are undoubtedly forgeries and therefore of no help to serious Ripperologists at all. As Abberline himself said, the writing of memoirs by mere inspectors was frowned upon by the Met hierarchy - the more the pity for us, because valuable information was simply never committed to paper.

Inspector Frederick George Abberline was probably nearest to the Ripper as investigating officer on the spot. In later life he became convinced that the killer was Severin Klosowski, alias George Chapman.

Superintendent Thomas Arnold was Abberline's immediate boss as the man in charge of Whitechapels's CID.

Superintendent Thomas Arnold, as Head of H Division, should be as central a character as Abberline, but in fact he was on leave until the 'double event' and an interview he gave to the Eastern Press in 1893 makes it clear that he had no clue who the Ripper was. He had first joined the Met in 1855, but resigned to serve in the latter stages of the Crimean War and rejoined in 1856. He knew the East End better than Abberline and was involved in the arrest and trial of Israel Lipski, a Polish immigrant umbrella-maker who poisoned Miriam Angel with nitric acid in 1887. To lasting condemnation by Ripperologists, it was Arnold who suggested to Warren that the Goulston Street writing should be erased. Interestingly, Arnold believed that only four of the five victims were the targets of Jack the Ripper, but a piece of bad reporting in 1893 doesn't make it clear whether he was excluding Kate Eddowes or Mary Kelly from the list.

Chief Inspector Donald Swanson is an altogether more important figure than Arnold. Like a large number of London detectives, originally from Scotland, he joined the Met in 1868 after realizing what a dead end job teaching was and by November 1887 was Chief Inspector of the CID at the Yard. This made him the most senior detective involved with the case at close quarters. Like other detectives, Swanson had been heavily engaged against the Fenians in the 1870s and 1880s; a bomb was even placed in Scotland Yard itself at one point. He was also famous as the officer to arrest Percy Le Froy, the railway murderer, in 1881.

Swanson was a personal friend of Dr Robert Anderson and in a copy of Anderson's book *The Lighter Side of my Official Life*, published in 1910, the retired Chief Inspector wrote pencilled notes which were not discovered until the 1980s. In it he names the suspect hinted at in print by Anderson. The rest is silence.

Historian Philip Sugden, in his definitive *The Complete History of Jack the Ripper*, claims that the political infighting of Swanson's superiors, right up to the Home Secretary, is largely irrelevant to the Ripper case. This would be true

Chief Inspector Donald Swanson - 'a very capable officer with a synthetical turn of mind' - whose Scottish education set him apart from most officers who came up the hard way.

Major Henry Smith, seen here in old age, was Acting Commissioner of the City Force in 1888. As a good PR man, he suffered less at the hands of the press than many of his Met colleagues.

were it not for the fact that the infighting proves the astonishing arrogance and incompetence of the men who ultimately made the decisions which did relate to the case.

For practical purposes, the most senior man in the City Force was Major Henry Smith, an Edinburgh University graduate who was Acting Commissioner when Kate Eddowes died on his 'manor'. He was a good PR man (at a time when most policemen had no inkling how useful it was to have the press on their side) and the City Force seems to have been held in higher regard than the Met by all and sundry. In his memoirs *From Constable to Commissioner*, which appeared in the same year as Anderson's book, he wrote, 'There is no man living who knows as much of these murders as I do.' Unfortunately, a considerable number of Smith's anecdotes are demonstrably false. He claims to have been 'within five minutes of the perpetrator one night' and uses the same phrase to cover the murders in Mitre Square and Miller's Court. Even the title of his book is nonsense - Smith entered the force with a senior rank and had never been a constable in his life. He attacked Warren of the Met for destroying the Goulston Street writing and Robert Anderson for claiming to know who the Ripper was. One of the few honest things he wrote was 'I must admit . . . [The Ripper] completely beat me and every police officer in London.' It is likely to have been Smith's decision not to co-operate with the Met. His report to Matthews, the Home Secretary, was unhelpful to the point of secrecy. This was no way to conduct a murder enquiry and Robert Peel, who had failed to tackle the City police in 1829, must have turned in his grave.

James Monro, another leading Scotsman in the Yard corridors of power. A devout Christian, he championed the cause of his constables in their long fight for better pay and conditions of service.

The senior organization of the Met is more complicated and here we are concerned with four men under Henry Matthews, the Home Secretary. The first is Assistant Commissioner James Monro, like Smith an Edinburgh University man and with experience in the Indian police of the Bombay Presidency. A devout Christian and strict martinet (like his colleagues Anderson and Warren), he was (unlike them) enormously popular. It is a fact, however, that Monro was stubborn and difficult. In 1887 he took over the running of a new Department at the Yard - Department D - which was specifically created to cope with the rising tide of potential anarchy occasioned by the Irish Fenians and the influx of Eastern Europeans. In time, this Praetorian Guard of detectives, whom Monro regarded as the 'crème de la crème', would become the Special Branch. Then, however, it was 'Monro's Secret Department' and Warren resented its existence. Monro never went into print on the Ripper case, although he was regularly updated on progress by various superintendents throughout September 1888 and presumably knew as much as any senior policeman. In one very telling phrase to his grandson

Sir Robert Anderson, Assistant Commissioner, CID, in a photograph taken years later. A lawyer and prolific writer, H.L. Adam, said of him 'What he did not know about crime was scarcely knowledge.' Even so, he was wrong about Jack.

after his retirement, Monro said 'the Ripper was never caught, but he should have been.'

From October 6 of the Autumn of Terror, the man in charge of the Ripper case was Dr Robert Anderson. An Irish-born lawyer, Anderson was closely involved against the Fenians in the 1880s and was appointed Assistant Commissioner at the Met on the day Polly Nichols died. It was particularly unfortunate that on the day of Annie Chapman's murder he left for Switzerland on sick leave and did not return until after the 'double event'. The Victorians were obsessed with fresh air and complete rest (cures only available to the wealthy) and Anderson has not impressed later commentators by his lily-livered disappearance at the most crucial moment of his career. Some authorities say that at one point he moved to Paris in order to be nearer to the appalling events in the Abyss!

Anderson was criticized later when his memoirs appeared, because he struck an anti-Semitic note:

> And the conclusion we came to was that he and his people were low-class Jews, for it is a remarkable fact that people of that class in the East End will not give up any of their number to Gentile justice.

With Anderson, as with Smith, we have this astonishing arrogance which pervades their memoirs. The memoirs themselves of course were written years after the events and that alone makes them suspect to historians.

The spy cartoon of Melville McNaghten, Assistant Commissioner at the Yard, after the Whitechapel murders. Popular, quick-witted and intelligent, the three names of suspects he left in his Memoranda can now be eliminated.

Melville McNaghten was the son of the last chairman of the Honourable East India Company, and educated at Eton. Before his appointment as Assistant Chief Constable, CID, at Scotland Yard he managed his father's tea plantations in India and met James Monro there. The fact that McNaghten had been attacked by Indian land rioters was an automatic slur against him as far as Charles Warren was concerned. The Commissioner objected to McNaghten's appointment because he was 'the only man in India to be beaten by Hindoos.' Consequently, it was not until Warren's resignation, on the day Mary Kelly's body was found, that McNaghten came into the picture. In fact, he didn't take up his appointment until June 1889, eight months after the last killing. But this urbane and charming policeman (the first Assistant Commissioner to make an arrest of a burglar, according to *Vanity Fair*) is important because of the papers he left to his daughter. Now known as the 'McNaghten Memoranda', they have been exhaustively researched. 'Of course [the Ripper] was a maniac,' McNaghten told the *Daily Mail* on his retirement, 'but I have a very clear idea who he was and how he committed suicide, but that, with other secrets, will never be revealed by me.'

Not without reason, it is Sir Charles Warren who has come in for most criticism in connection with the Ripper murders. He was one in a long line of senior officers recruited from the army, obtaining a commission in the Royal Engineers in 1857 and served largely in Africa (including the General Gordon relief force in 1885) before recall to England to replace Edward Henderson as Commissioner of the Metropolitan Police. Though popular at first - the *Times* reported in its editorial that Warren was 'precisely the man whom sensible Londoners would have chosen to preside over the police of the Metropolis' - his intolerant militarism and mishandling of working class demonstrations reversed this situation. As an army man, Warren expected instant obedience from everyone under his command. Instead, he found Monro largely a law unto himself and was constantly at loggerheads with politicians like Henry Matthews and civil servants like Geoffrey Lushington, Permanent Under-Secretary at the Home Office.

Two of the silliest ideas used in the Ripper case - photographing the eyes of Kate Eddowes and the use of bloodhounds - were given the go-ahead by him. The idea of the photographs (see this book's cover) was that there was a 'scientific' belief abroad at the time that the exposed negative would reveal the last sight seen by the victim, stamped on the retina - in other words, a perfect 'fish eye' shot of Jack in the act. Whether this was ever actually carried out is unknown, but it speaks volumes for the desperation of Warren and the Met that it was even considered. The bloodhounds idea came from letters to the *Times* (then the most important yardstick of educated opinion) and Edwin Brough, a dog breeder from Scarborough, brought two of his animals, Barnaby and Burgho, who carried out police trials in Regent's Park on October 9. The next day, in Hyde Park, with Warren himself playing the part of the 'fox', the results were less successful. The dogs did not actually bite Warren or get lost (two classic examples of Ripper mythology) but they couldn't handle scents in the stinking streets of Whitechapel. Such was the lack of communication in the Met that detectives stood outside Mary

Bloodhounds belonging to Edwin Brough being put through their paces by the Metropolitan Police in Hyde Park.

Sir Charles Warren, Commissioner of Metropolitan Police. No amount of revisionist whitewash can restore the reputation of this man. A military martinet, he had no experience whatever of the criminal mind and was utterly out of his depth against Jack.

Kelly's murder room at Miller's Court for two hours, unsure whether the dogs would be brought in or not.

In fact Warren had resigned and this became public knowledge on the day of the Kelly murder. It was widely believed that her death had prompted the resignation. The radical *Star* was triumphant - 'Whitechapel has avenged us for Bloody Sunday' - which wasn't actually true. Warren returned to the army where despite the glowing eulogy of him in *Celebrities of the Army*, published in 1902, he was involved in the appalling debacle and slaughter of Spion Kop.

Presiding over the Met was the Right Honourable Henry Matthews, the first Catholic to reach the Cabinet since the Reformation. He was not popular in political circles, regarded as something of a lightweight and was criticized for letting two Commissioners of Police (Warren and Monro) go within two years of each other. Civil servant Evelyn Ruggles-Brise wrote that Matthews was 'quite incapable of dealing with men'. He clashed later with the dashing and popular Colonel Edward Bradford, who replaced Warren and, as Ruggles-Brise said, '. . . if you couldn't get on with Bradford you could get on with nobody.' Contrary to common sense, Matthews refused to consider the idea of official rewards, believing that nothing but false information would be the likely result. Under continued pressure, he finally agreed to a pardon for various people involved in Mary Kelly's murder, obviously believing it to be the work of more than one killer. His reasons for this are unknown.

Recent writers on the Ripper murders, most notably Paul Begg, Martin Fido and Keith Skinner, have sought to whitewash the police of the day by pointing out that Jack was a new kind of criminal, that they had essentially no forensic science on their side and that the actions they took were at all times sensible and thorough. I cannot share this view. The Ripper was no magician, no phantom of the night. He was clever, resourceful and knew both the area and the shortcomings of the police very well. From the political infighting at the very top of the chain of command to the barely adequate coppers on the beat, the Metropolitan and City forces conspired, through stupidity and missed opportunities, to let Jack go free. The only section of the police force which emerges with some credit from the case is the 'middle management' level of detective inspectors and superintendents - men like Swanson and Abberline. At either end of the chain, men like Sir Charles Warren, the Commissioner of the Metropolitan Police; and Constable 881 Edward Watkins who saw nothing suspicious going on in Mitre Square while Kate Eddowes was being butchered, were lamentable in their respective neglect of duty.

Henry Matthews, Home Secretary and the first Catholic to hold cabinet rank since the Reformation 9 (when there was no cabinet!). As ultimate head of the Metropolitan Police, he provided an ineffectual lead.

YOURS TRULY

I'm not a butcher,
I'm not a Yid,
Nor yet a foreign skipper,
But I'm your own light-hearted friend,
Yours truly, Jack the Ripper.

YOURS TRULY

In 1891 a little board game for children appeared on the market. It was called 'How To Catch Jack' and, with varying degrees of sophistication, people have been playing it ever since! I am unaware of any definitive list of Ripper suspects, but it grows steadily longer, year by year.

Try it yourself. Take any named individual connected with the case - for example George Hutchinson, who remembered Mary Kelly's last client so well; or Joe Barnett, who lived and quarrelled with her; or Michael Kidney, the violent lover of Liz Stride; or Doctor Barnardo, who talked to her in the kitchen of the dosshouse at Number 32 'Flowery Dean' - and you can build a case against them. In the case of the men I've mentioned, it's already been done.

It is precisely because of the flippancy with which this has been carried out over the years that genuine crime historians have become disgusted with 'Ripperologists', some of whom are happy to bend old truths or invent new ones to point a finger at their favourite suspect.

But this is precisely what *The Many Faces of Jack the Ripper* is all about. Jack is now the 'universal man' of serial slaughter - he is all things to all men. The major problem is categorization. For sanity's sake I have divided this chapter into seven groups - Jews, Doctors, Visitors, Locals, Policeman, Others and Royals. 'Others' usually comes at the end of such a list but because each category contains contemporary (i.e. contemporary to the crimes) and modern suspects, the Royals must come last - there are no contemporary theories for them at all, which speaks volumes for their likely involvement. I have also scored each suspect with a figure between 0 and 10 (9 being highly plausible, 0 representing near-lunacy). A score of 10 would mean the Ripper's identity was proven. None of these suspects scares 10.

1. THE JEWS

God's 'chosen People' have been blamed by Gentiles for all sorts of crimes and abominations throughout history. In the 1880s, the streets of the Abyss were becoming the Ghetto with frightening rapidity. The 'original' inhabitants, the Irish-Cockneys I have called locals below, felt aggrieved and bewildered. It was almost certainly this deep-rooted racism, which went much further back than the recent influx of Eastern Europeans, which led to the scribblings on the wall in Goulston Street. It was generally believed that no native Londoner could be responsible for the appalling murders, so the killer was likely to have been found among the 'foreigners' whose alien babble, distinctive dress and appearance set them so far apart from the rest.

The journalist S. Gelberg wrote in 1903:

> If you would understand the immortal agony of Jewry, go into the East End colony . . . Its beshawled women with their pinched faces, its long-coated men with two thousand years of persecution stamped in their manner . . . the very Yiddish jargon itself which is scrawled on its walls and shop windows, as part of the grand passion of the chosen people.

a) John Pizer

John Pizer, known as 'Leather Apron', from a newspaper of 1888.

By September 5, less than a week after the murder of Polly Nichols, the press and the police were both looking for a character called 'Leather Apron'. He was aged about forty, thickset and bull-necked and wore, as no doubt even *Star* readers suspected from the nickname, a leather apron. There is some doubt whether this nickname referred to a particular individual or was merely a generic term for any slaughterman or tanner who wore such a garment as part of his trade. The Jewish slaughterhouses in the area specialized in the preparation of kosher food. In other words, the hated Jews carried knives in the street. And a knife had been used on Polly Nichols.

Anti-Semitic fury was whipped up quickly by the press. The *Star*, clobbering both the police and the Jews in one paragraph, gave the collar initials of the J Division officers who had had the 'crazy jew' in custody days earlier and had let him go. When a leather apron was found in the murder yard behind Number 29 Hanbury Street, the seething cauldron of the Abyss boiled over and Jews were beaten up on the streets.

The man they were all looking for was an unemployed slipper maker who drank at the Princess Alice and had a dosser friend called Mickeldy Joe. He had mad, staring eyes, a terrifying smile, carried knives, cudgels and a pistol and was known to have threatened and assaulted women. Descriptions like this, as well as being meat and drink to the press, were what Victorians expected to see in their murderers. The caricatures of criminals portrayed in *Punch*, with their apelike muzzles and Neanderthal foreheads were, to most of the magazine's readers, faithful representations. The People of the Abyss really did look like that. With our vastly greater experience, we know that serial killers have charm, wit and even strong physical charisma. Denis Neilson, Jeffrey Dahmer and Ted Bundy used charm and friendliness to get their victims where they wanted them.

On Monday, September 10, 'Johnny Upright' knocked on the door at Number 22 Mulberry Street. 'You're just the man I want,' said Sergeant Thick and arrested John Pizer, the leather worker who lived there. At an identification parade at Leman Street police station, Mrs Fiddymont, landlady of the 'clean house', the Prince Albert pub in Brushfield Street, who had seen a bloodstained man drinking in her premises on the evening of September 7, could not identify Pizer. Emmanuel Violena, a mulatto bootmaker who lodged in Hanbury Street, recognized Pizer as one of two men quarrelling with a woman in the early hours of September 8. Subsequent inquiries by the police brought the mulatto's evidence into question.

On Wednesday September 12 Pizer appeared at the inquest into Annie Chapman's murder. He had in fact an unshakeable alibi for the night of Polly Nichols' death when he slept in Crossman's lodging house in Holloway. A certain notoriety clung to the man, despite his having officially been cleared of the murders. He was hit over the head by Emily Patswold and her umbrella, for which she was fined 10 shillings. Pizer died of gastroenteritis in July 1897.

1

b) Joseph Isaacs

Many men were reported to the police in the Autumn of Terror because of their strange behaviour and Joseph Isaacs was one of these. A cigarmaker by profession, he lodged in Little Paternoster Row, a long-demolished street only yards from Miller's Court, and Mary Cusins, the keeper of the house, reported that Isaacs was heard pacing the floor of his room all night and that he left suddenly after the murder of Mary Kelly. He left a violin bow behind and came back for it on December 5 or 7.

Mary Cusins had been asked by the police to keep an eye out for Isaacs and she followed him to Julius Levenson's pawnshop (the man repaired instruments on the side). He was arrested in Drury Lane the next day and taken under escort to Leman Street station. Despite being interviewed by Abberline, his only apparent crime was that he had stolen a watch from Levenson's and was duly charged with that.

The questioning of Isaacs speaks volumes for the hysteria which had gripped the Abyss by the time of Mary Kelly's murder. 'The lodger' was borne of the idea that no one in the area (Isaacs had only been at Mary Cusins' lodging house for a few days) could be guilty of such repulsive crimes. The actual evidence against Isaacs is of course nonexistent. He was not known in the area and couldn't sleep - that is the sole extent of Mary Cusins' suspicions against him. The fact that he was interrogated by Abberline also suggests that the police were desperate by this stage and daren't leave any stone unturned.

0

c) Olga Tchkersoff

The likelihood of the Ripper being a woman is discussed elsewhere, but Olga is an unusual example of a suspect whose name appears nowhere in contemporary accounts, yet is not of the recent 'lunatic fringe' variety. Edwin Woodhall, a policeman born three years before Jack struck, points the finger at Olga in his *When London Walked In Terror* (1937).

   Via a rather tortuous journalistic route, Olga is supposed to have told her story to fellow Russian immigrants and Woodhall evidently read a version of this somewhere. There is no actual evidence that Olga was Jewish, but she was a recent immigrant from Russia in the 1880s and her sister, Vera, a prostitute, died as a result of an abortion (which was of course illegal in 1888). It was Mary Kelly (whom Woodhall oddly calls Marie Taylor) who tempted Vera into a life on the streets in the first place. This does not of course explain the other murders and the Ripper being female raises a host of difficulties.

0

d) Aaron Cohen

On December 7 1888, Aaron Davis Cohen was brought before Thames magistrates court as a 'lunatic wandering at large'. The number of such people in the Abyss must be a matter of conjecture, but Jack London estimates nearly half a million inhabitants altogether. In that number, there must have been a reasonable percentage who were unstable or mentally ill in one way or another. Bad diet and lack of state care would probably have meant that this percentage was quite large. Certainly we meet a lot of them as potential Rippers, of whom their neighbours were suspicious; and because they were reported to the police, this gives the impression of a greater concentration still.

The magistrates sent Cohen to the 'Spike' Infirmary where he gave the name David Cohen. He was twenty-three years old and lived in Leman Street with no family known. His behaviour at the 'Spike' was violent. Whereas Jack London ran away from its grimness, Cohen damaged the furniture (such as it was) and attacked other inmates. On December 21 he was transferred to Colney Hatch, the County Asylum. His wild behaviour continued there and he had to be force-fed. His physical condition deteriorated in the following months and he died of exhaustion and pulmonary tuberculosis on October 20 1889.

If we assume that serial killers cannot control their impulse to kill then according to a misunderstood convention, *something* had to remove Jack from the Abyss after November 9 1888. This pattern fits Cohen quite well, giving him only a month to wander without another victim. His address in Leman Street would be close enough to the Abyss for him to know the area well. Historian and criminologist Martin Fido believes that Cohen is the suspect referred to by Dr Robert Anderson, who in *The Lighter Side of my Official Life,* having maligned 'low class Jews' generally, goes on:

> I will add that when the individual whom we suspected was caged in an asylum, the only person who had ever had a good view of the murderer at once identified him, but when he learned that the suspect was a fellow-Jew he declined to swear to him.

This archness on Anderson's part - 'Having regard to the interest attaching to this case, I should almost be tempted to disclose the identity of the murderer' - is infuriating. Martin Fido has taken it seriously and having searched the records for the relevant period, comes up with Cohen as the only possibility. That assumes, of course, that Anderson is right - and we have no way of knowing that.

Even so, with our knowledge of serial killers, the drooling, wandering, sad Aaron Cohen, does not fit the bill. A will 'o the wisp one moment, eluding 1500 policemen and an unknown number of vigilant amateurs, descends into a raving madman who is taken to court by a solitary constable? I think not.

1

e) Aaron Kosminski

The Polish hairdresser who arrived in London six years before the Autumn of Terror holds a prominence today among Ripper suspects. To begin with, various known facts about Kosminski fits him in Anderson's memoirs as neatly as Cohen. More directly, he is listed in Melville McNaghten's famous memoranda as suspect Number 2.

> Kosminski, a Polish Jew, who lived in the very heart of the district where the murders were committed. He had become insane owing to many years indulgence in solitary vices. He had a great hatred of women, with strong homicidal tendencies. He was (and I believe still is) detained in a lunatic asylum about March 1889. This man in appearance strongly resembled the individual seen by the City PC near Mitre Square.

What do we know about him? Kosminski entered the Mile End Old Town Workhouse on July 12 1890. Able bodied but insane, he was discharged into the care of his brother Wolf of Number 3, Sion Square. He was admitted to Colney Hatch on February 7 of the following year. The details of Kosminski's mental state have been admirably researched by Philip Sugden. The doctor who committed Kosminski wrote:

> He declares that he is guided and his movements altogether controlled by an instinct that informs his mind; he says that he knows the movements of all mankind; he refuses food from others because he is told to do so and eats out of the gutter for the same reason.

During the trial of Peter Sutcliffe, the Yorkshire Ripper, he also claimed to be driven to do what he did. His voices, he said, came from God. With the exception of one known incident, in which Kosminski threatened an attendant with a chairleg, his time both at Colney Hatch and Leavesden Home for Imbeciles, was remarkably quiet. He refused to work, muttered incomprehensibly and kept himself relatively clean after refusing at first to bathe.

McNaghten's assertion that Kosminski's mental state was the result of 'solitary vices' (masturbation) tells us a great deal about the Victorian layman's view of the perfectly normal and harmless habit. All the more sad that the occasional note from the Colney Hatch records says the same thing - 'self abuse'. The Victorians believed that insanity was the only outcome of masturbation and the anonymous author of *Walter: My Secret Life* was terrified of giving way to temptation when a girl wasn't available.

McNaghten in fact is notoriously inaccurate and makes mistakes all over the place. In his autobiography, he gives the reason - again, the mark of a senior policeman's arrogance:

> I never kept a diary, nor even possessed a notebook, so that . . . I must trust to my memory . . . alone.

And not for one moment did McNaghten believe that his memory could be wrong. No 'City PC' saw anyone near Mitre Square at the time of Kate Eddowes' murder. The only possible witness was the civilian Joseph Lawende and he admitted he wouldn't know the man again. Chief Inspector Swanson tells us that the identification took place (and exactly why is explained nowhere) at the 'seaside home', the Convalescent Police Home at Clarendon Villas in Hove. Swanson says the identification took place before Kosminski was sent to Colney Hatch, but as the Police Home wasn't opened until March 1890, this cannot be the case. In other words, Joseph Lawende was being asked to identify a man he saw briefly in the dark a *minimum* of seventeen months earlier. According to Anderson, Lawende (if that is indeed his witness) '*at once* identified him.'

In later years, McNaghten and Abberline both veered away from Kosminski. McNaghten favoured the barrister Montague Druitt; Abberline admitting openly in 1903 that 'Scotland Yard is really no wiser on the subject than it was fifteen years ago'. Kosminski was said to have threatened his sister with a knife - if he did, we have only to look to Jack London or Frederick Charrington to know that violence of this kind was a commonplace in the Abyss, rarely even coming to court. Apart from the incident with the chair, Kosminski showed no displays of violence and was never reported as being anti-women. He had no knowledge of anatomy. He was at liberty, picking up scraps from the gutter, for nearly two years after the murder of Mary Kelly.

None of it is enough to place a noose around the hairdresser's neck.

2

The fact that the Jews were believed to be guilty at all relates purely to the anti-Semitism of the Abyss in the 1880s. All the evidence shows that the Jews were obedient to the Talmud, the law. If the law frowned on prostitution, the law would provide retribution through God. It was not for any Jew to take the law into his own hands. The more Orthodox the Jew (in other words the more alien and unacceptable he was to the Gentiles of the Abyss) the less likely he was to have been Jack the Ripper. Of course, there are aberrations in any religious or racial group, but the pattern of modern serial killers is to target one of their own kind. If this held good in 1888, Jack would have killed Jewish women, not the five he did.

To take certain liberties with the Goulston Street scribblings, 'The Jews are not the men to be blamed.'

2. THE DOCTORS

Of the medical men who examined or carried out post-mortems on the bodies of Jack's victims, only Thomas Bond, involved in the Mary Kelly case, believed the murderer to have no anatomical knowledge. This is presumably because Mary's body was such a mess that no skill could be discerned. In the case of Annie Chapman and Kate Eddowes however, with wombs and kidneys removed, a lack of skill is patent nonsense.

What has never been agreed is the degree of anatomical knowledge necessary to account for the victims' wounds. Was the Ripper a slaughterman, a hunter (in the East End?) or a surgeon?

As we saw in the introduction to this book, the image we have of Jack is the toff, the 'swell', the caped and top-hatted man-about-town. That makes him all the more interesting and all the more sinister to us today. So the idea of the Ripper being a middle or upper class gent with a university education, medical training and respectability, is a more delicious prospect than a wandering lunatic from the Abyss.

a) Thomas Neill Cream.

There is no shortage of murderous doctors. Most of them kill for financial gain and use any one of the large variety of poisons they have access to. One of the least savoury of these was Dr Cream, the Lambeth Poisoner, although his motive was different.

Born in Glasgow in 1850, cross-eyed Cream graduated from McGill University, Canada in 1876. He practised medicine in Chicago but under the outward respectability was a vicious and deeply disturbed personality. Unlike the real Ripper, Cream was a self-publicist. He had an affair with a Mrs Stott, murdered her husband with strychnine in 1881 and could not resist writing to the District Attorney with the suggestion that Stott's body be exhumed. This apparently suicidal act led to his imprisonment in Joliet from where he was released in July 1891.

Over the next few months he fed strychnine pills to Lambeth prostitutes Ellen Donworth, Matilda Clover, Emma Shivell and Alice Marsh, before publicly offering to name the Lambeth Poisoner for £300,000. He was arrested in June 1892 and found guilty of murder in less than twelve minutes once the jury had begun their deliberations.

Dr Thomas Neill Cream, poisoner and sadist, whose strangled cry on the gallows led to speculation that he was the Ripper.

What, then, is the case for Cream being the Ripper? Virtually none. At the time of course, some of the bragging, taunting letters sent to newspapers and the police were still being taken seriously and Cream's behaviour follows this pattern. The most tantalizing piece of 'evidence' was his cry from under the billowing white hood as Thomas Billington slipped the noose around his neck and pulled the lever, jolting the perverted doctor into eternity - 'I am Jack the . . .'

Serial killers have been known to change their M.O. - in Cream's case, it would have been from poison to the knife, but it is unusual. What takes Cream out of the frame, of course, is his watertight alibi. He was still in Joliet prison in the Autumn of Terror and ludicrous theories about him escaping or bribing his way out do not ring true.

0

b) John Sanders

Though not technically a doctor, Sanders was the son of an Indian Army surgeon and was a student at the London Hospital (near Berner Street) in 1879. In 1881 however, he 'became ill and was placed in an asylum'. In 1887, increasingly violent and disturbed, he was sent to Holloway Asylum in Virginia Water and then to Heavitree, Essex, where he stayed until his death in 1901.

Although the press didn't get wind of it, Abberline and his team of detectives were trying to trace three insane medical students, all from the London Hospital, in late October 1888. Abberline had visited Sanders' home at Abercorn Place, Maida Vale and discovered that the man's mother had gone, but Sanders himself was probably already in Holloway Asylum by then. The dates of his admission are unknown, but Abberline took no further action, implying that Sanders had an alibi brought about by incarceration.

I must admit that the three insane medical students sound a little like the three stooges of a later generation and I find it bizarre that Warren and Swanson of the Met and Major Smith of the City Force should waste time on them. Two of these men (presumably including Sanders) were traced; the third had gone abroad. What are the odds against the London Hospital having three mad students at the same time?

0

c) Morgan Davies

Despite the Welsh-sounding name, Davies was born in Whitechapel and was a surgeon at the London Hospital. He was accused by a man who is himself a suspect, Robert Donston

Stephenson, who claimed to have seen Davies describe at a lecture at the hospital how the Ripper sodomized and murdered his victims. Stephenson also claimed that the journalist William T. Stead had told him that Mary Kelly had indeed been sodomized.

Stephenson was a notorious liar - I shall be dismissing the claim that he was the Ripper below. In other words, we have only the word of a deeply disturbed crank made against a perfectly ordinary and respectable member of the medical profession. There is of course no evidence that any of the Ripper victims was sodomized before or after death.

0

d) Oswald Puckridge

On September 19 1888, Sir Charles Warren wrote to the Home Secretary to tell him about progress on the Ripper case (notice that Warren had to be asked for this information - he did not volunteer it) and as well as the insane pork butcher Jacob Isenschmid (see under 'Others'), the Commissioner referred to:

> a man called Puckridge [who] was released from an asylum on 4 August. He was educated as a surgeon and has threatened to rip people up with a long knife.

Oswald Puckridge was born at Burpham, near Arundel, in 1838, which automatically makes him rather old, both for the classic profile of a serial killer and any of the known sightings. When he married Ellen Puddle, a victualler's daughter, in 1868, he gave his occupation as 'apothecary' (chemist). After a number of stays in various institutions (he was released from Hoxton House, a private asylum in Shoreditch on the date Warren gives above) he died in the Holborn Workhouse in City Road in June 1900 from pneumonia. His death certificate describes him as a general labourer.

All other information on Puckridge has gone, lost in the passing of the years. We have no idea if he had any medical training at all, how genuinely dangerous he was or whether he had any links with Whitechapel. At the time of Warren's memorandum, the police couldn't find him, yet we know he lived for twelve years after the Ripper case. Perhaps they did find him together with a firm alibi and so his file was closed.

1

e) 'Dr Stanley'

There is no doubt that two overriding considerations guided the police enquiries at the time - medical skill and insanity. In the case of 'Dr Stanley' however, we move forward from 1888 and into the realms of fiction which have dogged the Ripper murders almost from the beginning. The name crops up in *The Mystery of Jack the Ripper* by Leonard Matters in 1926.

'Stanley' was supposedly a doctor at a London hospital, which may have been Charing Cross and with a private practice at his house in Portman Square. At some time he was anaesthetist to Joseph Lister, the father of anaesthetics. His son Herbert went to bed with Mary Kelly on Boat Race Night 1886, contracted syphilis and died. 'Stanley' killed Kelly and her friends and fled to travel the world, reaching Buenos Aires where he died about 1918.

Various versions of this story had in fact been circulating long before Leonard Matters went into print. The *East London Observer* mentioned a similar tale as early as October 13 1888.

There are a number of objections to this theory, although it has survived in one form or another to the present day. The use of an alias - there is no Dr Stanley in the surviving medical records of any London hospital, nor as resident in Portman Square - immediately arouses suspicions. How did Herbert meet Mary Kelly in time for Boat Race night 1886 when she was living with plasterer Joseph Fleming in Bethnal Green at the time? Syphilis, before AIDS, was the only fatal venereal disease. Fatalities however usually take far longer than two years - in the case of Al Capone, for example, at least thirteen. Then, if 'Stanley' was intent on killing Mary Kelly, why kill her friends as well, in that each time he used his knife, he increased the chances of his being caught before he could reach his 'real' target in Miller's Court? We have no evidence (unlike Liz Stride) that Mary was syphilitic. Neither do we have conclusive proof that Jack's five victims actually did know each other.

American true crime writer Edward Pearson has put the 'Dr Stanley' theory neatly into perspective. It bears 'about the same relation to the facts of criminology as the exploits of Peter Rabbit and Jeremy Muskrat do to zoology.'

0

f) Frederick Chapman

The search for a 'mad doctor' has driven recent theorists to search medical historical records to find someone who fits in terms of known dates, behaviour and so on. B.E. Reilly, writing in City (the organ of the City of London Police), identified Chapman, who for some reason he called 'Dr Merchant' in 1972. Chapman qualified as a doctor in Glasgow in 1874 and came to London two years before the Ripper killings. He wrote a number of medical articles before his death in 1888 from a septic tubercular abscess.

It is possible that Chapman is referred to by Constable 101H Robert Spicer who claimed in 1931 that he had arrested a man with a prostitute called Rosie in Heneage Court off Brick Lane after the 'double event':

> He turned out to be a highly respected doctor and gave a Brixton address. His shirt cuffs still had blood on them. Jack had the proverbial bag with him . . . This was not opened and he was allowed to go . . . He was always dressed the same - high hat, black suit with silk facings and a gold watch and chain. He was about 5 feet 8 or 9 inches and about 12 stone, fair moustache, high forehead and rosy cheeks.

Spicer got into trouble for this arrest and was told by his superiors to leave well alone. If Chapman was 'slumming' and had a penchant for East End whores, he would not be unique, but again, the Chapman theory is riddled with holes. It is likely that he was very ill for some time before his death. Would he have been physically strong enough to kill and mutilate five women with the speed and ferocity with which we know Jack worked? Chapman lived in Brixton, south of the river. Other than Spicer (who of course gives no names) we have nothing that links him with Whitechapel. And what of Spicer's report? It was made forty three years after the event and by a man who was dismissed in 1889 as being 'unfit for police service'. The fact that he stated that the Brixton doctor was still accosting prostitutes in Liverpool Street station some time later rules Chapman out. He was dead by then.

1

g) William Wynn Westcott

A misreading of the clues left at various Ripper murder sites, especially the disembowelling, the arrangement of the coins beside Annie Chapman and even the choice of site in the case of Kate Eddowes has led various theorists to see an element of ritual in the killings. This notion reached its most elaborate (and absurd) stage in the 'final solution' of journalist Stephen Knight in 1976.

William Wynn Westcott is another contender, however, because he not only had medical skills, but was a member of the Order of the Golden Dawn which he joined shortly before the Ripper killings.

Westcott trained at University College, London (from its premises in Gower Street, he may have been familiar with the Abyss as a young man), practised in the West Country near Yeovil and moved to Camden (seriously out of the way of the Abyss) in 1887 as Coroner for Central London. Dennis Wheatley, in *The Devil and All His Works*, lists the famous members of the Golden Dawn, an occult society with Rosicrucian leanings. McGregor Matthews had founded it, but Algernon Blackwood, the Gothic story writer, W.B. Yeats, the poet and Aleister Crowley, 'The Beast' (who claimed to know who the Ripper was, incidentally) - are far better known.

Westcott had no obvious links with Whitechapel, was never known to be misogynistic or violent and the whole claim is highly spurious. The whole idea of linking the Golden Dawn to serial murder is as far fetched as Stephen Knight's better known Masonic connection.

0

h) Sir William Gull - see under 'The Royals'

i) Francis Tumblety - see under 'Visitors'

3. THE VISITORS

Polly Nichols died in the early hours of Saturday 31 August; Annie Chapman on Saturday September 8; Liz Stride and Kate Eddowes on Saturday/Sunday September 30 and Mary Kelly on Friday November 9. The killings unmistakably followed a pattern. Jack always struck on a Friday or Saturday night. In modern psychology that tells us a lot about him. In 1888 it meant almost nothing. There were eight days between the first two murders, twenty-two between the second and the 'double event', forty between that and the last. Such a pattern seemed random to the Victorian police. It has more significance for us now.

Even so, the chauvinism persisted. No Englishman (perhaps not even an alien Jew living in England) could commit such appalling crimes, but Whitechapel was only a short walk from the docks. The wagons from Commercial Road trundled there in the early hours of every morning. What more natural than a crewman of a visiting merchant ship in the busiest docks in the world? Foreigners were capable of unspeakable acts, Englishmen believed, and the killer would be gone on the next tide.

a) Nikaner Benelius

Benelius was not a 'foreign skipper' but a Swedish traveller in London whose behaviour was decidedly odd. On the morning of November 17 1888, eleven days after Mary Kelly died, he walked unannounced into the front room of Mrs Harriet Rowe of Buxton Street, Mile End. When she asked him what he wanted, he leered at her and left. She followed him outside and found him in conversation with a passing policeman (who says there's never one about?), Constable Henry Imhoff of H Division. The stranger was asking directions to Fenchurch Street Post Office when Mrs Rowe blurted out to Imhoff what had happened. The Swede was promptly arrested.

Benelius gave his address as Great Eastern Street, Shoreditch, and he was charged with entering a dwelling house for an unlawful purpose. In fact, the police had met him already. Constable Walter Dew, also of H Division, who went on to become one of the celebrities of the Yard as the man who caught Crippen in 1910, said that Benelius had been interviewed after the murder of fellow-Swede Liz Stride. The man was prone to wander the streets preaching. He carried no weapons, had offered no violence and probably seeing Mrs Rowe's door open had merely gone in to ask directions. Two days after his arrest, the police let him go.

0

b) José Laurenco, Manuel Xavier, Joao Machado and Joachim de Rocha

This is one of the most interesting pieces of contemporary speculation. It is unique in that it represents a sort of folie à deux, not in the sense that two sailors worked together, but that one copied the butchery of the other, and this was relayed to two more!

Edward Larkins seems to have been a busybody who worked as a clerk in the Statistical Department of Customs and Excise. As such, his knowledge of comings and goings at the docks may well have been encyclopedic. On November 12 1888 he gave the police the name Antoni Pricha as one who resembled the foreign looking man described by George Hutchinson going into Miller's Court with Mary Kelly four days earlier. Not content with that, Larkins watched carefully the Portuguese cattle boats City of London and City of Oporto. He had read accounts of atrocities committed on French troops by Portuguese partisans in the Peninsular War (1808-14). The Spanish court painter Goya shows limbs cut off, decorating the shrubbery. Guerillas swept from the mountains onto unsuspecting French columns; stragglers had their genitals hacked off and rammed into their mouths as a token of ultimate contempt. Larkins clearly believed that such antisocial behaviour was constant Portuguese practice and he concluded that crew-member Manuel Cruz Xavier killed Polly Nichols while his ship was in port and that José Laurenco killed Annie Chapman in a copy cat murder the next time the ship was in (Xavier did not return a second time).

A third crewman, Joao de Souza Machado, was believed by Larkins to have worked with Laurenco on the murders of Annie Chapman, Liz Stride and Kate Eddowes and that Machado killed Kelly alone (in that Laurenco jumped ship at Opporto in October). Since Larkins believed that 'Clay Pipe' Alice McKenzie was also murdered by the Ripper on July 17 1889 and Machado was not on the ship on that date, he passed the buck to Joachim de Rocha, another crewman.

To give the police their due, they did follow up Larkins' half-baked enquiries, both in the Port of London and in Portugal. The answer was a firm blank. The idea of four homicidal maniacs serving on the same merchant ship defies belief and is even crankier than the three insane medical students of the London Hospital. Today, I have no doubt that Larkins would be charged with wasting police time.

0

c) William Piggott

Another sailor to be hauled in by the police, on Sunday September 9, was William Henry Piggott, a ship's cook. He was arrested in Gravesend with a gashed hand and was said to have been yelling his hatred of women in the Pope's Head pub. A parcel left behind by him at a fish and pie stall contained a torn and bloody shirt.

Piggott's excuse was that he had tried to help a woman who was having a fit in Whitechapel early on Saturday morning (September

8) and that she had bitten his hand, causing both the wound and the damage to the shirt. He was interviewed by Abberline and put in a line up to face Mrs Fiddymont, still at that stage intent on finding the bloody man in her pub, the 'clean house'. She couldn't identify him and Piggott was taken to the Spike infirmary where he was found to be suffering from delirium tremens (the shakes brought on by drink) and was released without charge on October 9.

Piggott is not in the same category as others in this section in that he was only a visitor from a short distance away (Gravesend). He knew the area because an earlier address for him is 19 Brick Lane. He seems to have fallen on hard times, like many who filtered down through the Abyss. Whether his apparent drink problem was a cause or a consequence of this, we'll never know, but there is nothing in Piggott to lead us to believe him to be Jack.

0

d) G. Wentworth Smith

Dr Lyttleton Forbes Winslow was educated at Rugby and Downing College, Cambridge. Both a doctor of medicine and of law, he regarded himself by the late 1880s as *the* expert on the issues of legal sanity (still in his day based on the M'Naghten rules named after the madman who had tried to kill Sir Robert Peel in 1843). He wrote *Handbook for Attendants on the Insane* and founded the British Hospital for Mental Disorders. He trumpeted the theory, at every opportunity, that the Ripper was a 'homicidal monomaniac of infinite cunning'. He believed he could catch the murderer with a team of six constables and offered his services to Sir James Fraser, of the City Police, on October 2 1888.

Forbes Winslow may have been, like Edward Larkins, an interfering busybody, albeit one with better credentials, but he was not just whistling in the pre-Freudian dark. He had a man in the frame - G. Wentworth Smith.

Smith was the representative of a Canadian firm, the Toronto Trust Society, and worked from an office in Godliman Street near St Paul's Cathedral. In the month before the Ripper struck he lodged at Number 27 Sun Street, Finsbury Square, in the home of Mr and Mrs Callaghan. Callaghan noted Smith's strange behaviour: he owned three revolvers, kept odd hours, wore rubber soled galoshes, talked to himself and seemed to be, in the words of one of the hoax Ripper letters, 'down on whores', complaining that they even wandered through St Paul's during services. Callaghan believed that Smith was on the streets on the

Dr Lyttleton Forbes Winslow, leading 'mad doctor' of his day, became convinced that he knew who the Ripper was.

night of Martha Tabram's murder, but when a female friend told him she had been accosted by a man months after Smith had left Callaghan's (and probably the country), Callaghan made the assumption that this was Smith. He certainly persuaded Forbes Winslow that Smith was 'without doubt the perpetrator of these crimes', but Chief Inspector Swanson was less impressed.

There was simply nothing to link Smith with Whitechapel, nor the use of knives nor any violent activity. It may even have been standard for Canadian insurance agents abroad to carry revolvers!

0

e) Alios Szemeredy and Nicolai Wassili

I place these two suspects together not because they worked in tandem, but because they are two examples of a classic type. We know of them only from allegations in foreign newspapers. The fact that do not appear on police files does not mean that they went unchecked at the time - many Scotland Yard files are missing.

Szemeredy appears in what is probably the first full-length book on the subject - *Hvem var Jack the Ripper?* - written by Dutchman Carl Muusmann in 1908. Some sixteen years earlier, Szemeredy was arrested in Vienna on suspicion of murder and committed suicide in police custody. He was known to the Austrian authorities because he deserted from the army and sailed to Buenos Aires where he may have committed a murder or murders. In 1885 he was in an asylum. Rumours circulating in Vienna that he was the Ripper were reported in the *London Daily Graphic* in 1892.

The case against Szemeredy would seem to be nonexistent. He may have had homicidal tendencies or even been a murderer and there seems little doubt he was deeply disturbed. However, links with Whitechapel or even Britain are highly dubious.

Nicolai Wassili may have visited the Abyss, but there is no actual proof that he did. He was born in Tiraspol in the Ukrainian Steppes in 1842 and attended the University of Odessa. Russia in the 19th century was full of superstition and wandering *staretzy* (holy men) of whom Grigori Rasputin (see Pedachenko below) is the most famous. Wassili joined one of the many fanatical sects which lay outside the Russian Orthodox church, the Shorn, who believed that all sexual relations were impure and taboo, even within marriage (as opposed to Rasputin's view that sexual sin was rather a good idea!).

When the Shorn were suppressed in 1872, Wassili went west to Paris and spent his time converting whores. He fell in love with one of them, Madeleine, and her rejection of him brought about a mental breakdown and released the urge to kill. He killed five women, coincidentally enough, but in a far smaller timescale than Jack and stabbed them all in the back without mutilation.

Released from an asylum in January 1888, he announced his intention of coming to Britain. It may be that Mrs Belloc Lowndes' classic *The Lodger* (from which several films have been made) is based on the Wassili story - her father was a French lawyer.

Again, as with Szemeredy, the case against Wassili is feeble. Most of the accounts of his murderous Parisian spree are from European papers who have copied each other with no attempt to verify the facts. Without tangible evidence that he was in the Abyss in the Autumn of Terror, we must relegate Wassili to the realms of improbability.

0

f) Alexei Pedachenko

Of all the modern theories on the identity of the Ripper, the case of Alexei Pedachenko alias Count Andrey Luiskovo alias (possibly) Wassili Konovalov must be the silliest. At least the 'mad doctor' myth was engendered by the apparent anatomical skills of the Ripper, but the 'mad Russian agent' makes absolutely no sense at all. Pedachenko first emerged in *The Identity of Jack the Ripper,* written by Donald McCormick in 1959 - in its day an enormously influential book. Pedachenko was born in Tver, Russia, in the late 1850s and worked in the hospital there (thereby giving him, presumably, medical training as well as access to surgeon's knives). He worked also for the Okhrana, the Tsarist secret police, and was described by them in 1888 as 'the greatest and boldest of all Russian criminal lunatics'. At that time, for reasons that are unclear, he lived in Walworth, South London, with his sister and it seems that he was used as some sort of maniacal hit man with the full backing of the Okhrana.

Pedachenko had two accomplices - a fellow Russian named Levitski who acted as lookout man while Pedachenko did the rippings and later wrote the Ripper letters; and a Miss Winberg, a tailoress from Walworth who engaged the luckless five in conversation in order not to arouse their suspicions until 'mad Alexei' turned up.

Pedachenko was smuggled out of London with the intention of exiling him (with Levitski) to Yakutsk in the wilderness of Siberia where he could do little harm. But killing had become a way of life with him and he was caught in the act of murder five months later and incarcerated in an asylum for life.

William Le Queux, the traveller and journalist who made the Russian connection with the Ripper. Unfortunately, he made most of it up.

It is possible that Pedachenko was a Russian surgeon named Wassili Konovalov, whose physical description could easily fit the 'foreign' looking man seen by George Hutchinson with Mary Kelly on the night she died. He was believed to have killed five prostitutes in Paris in 1887 before moving to London, although the similarity of names would imply confusion in the newspapers of the day with Nicolai Wassili (see above). A Parisian girl was indeed butchered in November 1886, her head, legs and right arm hacked from the torso and her uterus ripped out. The cord that the body was tied with (utterly unlike anything seen in the Whitechapel killings) was of English manufacture.

Dr Thomas Dutton was living at Number 130 Aldgate at the time of the murders and produced a 'Chronicle of Crime' which Donald McCormick used later. Part of the Pedachenko story came from him, but since Dutton claimed not only to have assisted at the Ripper post-mortems, been an advisor to Abberline and to have been a suspect himself, his 'theories' must be cause for some doubt.

The other source for Pedachenko is the lamentable William le Queux. A freelance journalist and third rate novelist, le Queux admitted that with two other journalists in 1888:

> We wrote up picturesque and lurid details while we stood on the very spot where the tragedy had occurred.

He was still making it up when he wrote *The Rascal Monk* in 1917, an almost purely fictitious account of Rasputin and the Empress Alexandra. Presumably his 1923 effort - *Things I Know About Kings, Celebrities and Crooks* - in which he claimed to have used secret Russian papers supplied by Rasputin, apparently in French, was equally spurious.

The only problem with this nonsense is where to begin to demolish it! Rasputin spoke no French, le Queux cannot be trusted, Dutton's 'Chronicles of Crime' (if they ever existed) have disappeared. It is now impossible to say whether Pedachenko and Konovalov are one man or two. The most serious caveat however is the total absence of motive. The Okhrana's purpose in sending Pedachenko across was to embarrass and discredit the British police because they allowed Russian dissidents to settle in the East End. While it is true that pogroms took place in Russian provinces and that Jews were distinctly unpopular there, the notion that Alexander III's government was so paranoid as to punish their asylum-givers seems cranky in the extreme.

g) Francis Tumblety

It was only a matter of time before the Americans got in on the act. Harold Schechter and David Everitt in the *A to Z Encyclopedia of Serial Killers* give a chilling statistic:

'Dr' Francis Tumbelty, the American quack and self-publicist, in typical pose with vast Dundrearies and a uniform and medals to which he was not entitled.

> nearly three quarters of all known serial killers in the world - 74 per cent, to be exact - come from the United States (as opposed to a measly 19% for all of Europe). Clealy there is something about American culture that is conducive to serial murder.

Two examples, both of them weak, will make the point. The first was a Norwegian sailor who was living in Jersey City (so I suppose he was only an honorary American!) and was incarcerated in Morris Plains Lunatic Asylum. His sole connection with the Ripper killings is that he collected newspaper cuttings on the case. The second is the confusingly named George Hutchinson (no relation to Mary Kelly's friend) who lived in Elgin, Illinois, and mutilated a woman in Chicago in the early 1880s, having escaped from an asylum. His whereabouts in 1889 when W.T. Stead's *Pall Mall Gazette* carried the story, were unknown.

Francis Tumblety is an altogether different proposition and is the most recent serious suspect to emerge. An Irishman, his family moved to Rochester, New York State when he was a child. He plied the canal boats as a teenager, hawking naughty books and learned herbalism somewhere along the way. America, far more than Britain, was the home of the quack in the 19th century and Tumblety set himself up as an 'electric doctor' in Detroit in 1854. After complaints and the death of at least one patient he moved on constantly.

In the hysteria surrounding John Brown's attempted slave rebellion in 1859 and the firing on Fort Sumter which led to the Civil War in 1861, Tumblety took to wearing elaborate hussar-style uniforms, pinning medals to his jacket and riding a grey horse. His delusions of grandeur included the claim that he was a surgeon with the Union Army and a personal friend of General Ulysses Grant and President Abraham Lincoln. Despite this, he was accused in 1865 of being involved in the conspiracy to murder Lincoln four days after the war ended. He printed, at his own cost, a public rebuttal of these charges on his release.

Travelling extensively, Tumblety was in London by November 1888 and was arrested there on November 7, charged with eight counts of gross indecency against men. He skipped bail and fled to France before his trial at the Old Bailey. Using the alias Frank

Townsend, he sailed to New York. Pursued by Inspector Walter Andrews, he vanished until the whole thing died down and once again emerged with vitriolic denials that he had any connection with the Ripper murders, which some American papers were claiming.

When Tumblety died in 1903, a collection of uteri was found in his St. Louis home.

Stewart Evans and Paul Gainey, two Suffolk policemen, list fifteen points in their *Jack the Ripper, First American Serial Killer* which they believe point to Tumblety's guilt. Unfortunately, virtually all of them are circumstantial and would not fulfil the requirements of the Crown Prosecution Service today, nor its equivalent in 1888.

The first point is that Tumblety 'fits many of the psychological requirements; he was a "psychopathia sexualis" subject'. As we shall see in the next chapter, modern profiling of serial killers is altogether different from Richard Kraft-Ebbing's pioneering work of 1886 and Tumblety fails to fit as many of the 'requirements' as he does fit. His supposed hatred of women - '[he] hated women, especially prostitutes, with a vengeance' - is commented on by some contemporaries, but others who knew him well refused to believe he was capable of such crimes.

Secondly, he was in London at the time, say Evans and Gainey, and 'had a good knowledge of the slums of the East End'. The theory was that the police were interested in an American who lodged at Number 22 Batty Street, near Berner Street where Liz Stride was killed and his landlady discovered one of his bloodstained shirts, which made her suspicious of him. There is of course no evidence whatever that the American's bloodstains belonged to a Ripper victim or that the lodger was Tumblety.

Thirdly, Tumblety owned a collection of uteri 'from all classes of women' and had anatomical knowledge. Tumblety was such an accomplished liar that his credentials are impossible to check. He claimed to have graduated from Dublin University and to have studied medicine in New York. Very little about him actually approximates with the truth. In other words, we have no idea whether he had any anatomical skills or not.

Fourth, 'he was arrested within days of the Kelly murder on suspicion of being the Whitechapel murderer'. The sole 'evidence' for this comes from American newspapers, the *New York Times* and the *New York World*, published three thousand miles away from events. There is nothing in the British press to suggest that this was why Tumblety was held and there is no mention of him whatsoever in the police files. He was actually arrested on November 7, two days before Mary Kelly was killed.

Evans and Gainey assume that he was bailed to wander the streets in search of her, but equally, he may have been in jail, which obviously rules him out completely. The circumstances of his arrest are vague. The *New York World* (December 2 1888) said that because the police had insufficient evidence to hold him on the Ripper killings, he was charged with:

> another offence against a statute which was passed shortly after the publication in the Pall Mall Gazette of 'The Maiden Tribute' and as a direct consequence thereof, Dr Tumblety was committed for trial.

'The Maiden Tribute' was W.T. Stead's outraged article on the availability of under age girls for sex but Tumblety fell foul of the same law that Oscar Wilde crashed before two years later - Henry Labouchere's Criminal Law Amendment Act, which outlawed homosexual activity. Tumblety's bail stood at £300 (which for all his supposed wealth he had to find bondsmen for) and the charge was of gross indecency with John Doughty, Arthur Brice, Albert Fisher and James Crowley. There seems little doubt then that Tumblety was homosexual, but the prudery of the Victorian press does not allow details.

'The murders ceased upon his arrest and subsequent flight', Evans and Gainey tell us, 'a very strong indicator.' Perhaps, but for nearly thirty years and for the same reason, fingers were pointed at M.J. Druitt, the barrister. In itself, it means nothing.

'A top Yard man felt he was the killer'. This is Chief Inspector John Littlechild, head of Monro's Secret Department, who wrote a letter to journalist George Sims in 1913. According to Littlechild, there was a large dossier on him at the Yard, but the Special Branch man admits that Tumblety was not considered a sadist. Again, there is no hint here of Tumblety's arrest for anything other than gross indecency with other men. Littlechild believed Tumblety to be a likely suspect, but it is certainly odd that no other policeman mentions him and that the London press, who so avidly followed the Ripper case at every twist, should not get wind of the story.

Tumblety used aliases and was 'always turning up and disappearing again', Evans and Gainey say. Probably well over half the people of the Abyss used aliases, let alone shifty American con-men. A slippery, streetwise character, as Tumblety undoubtedly was, does not make a typical serial killer.

Inspector John Littlechild, Head of Monro's Secret Department (later, Special Branch) who believed Tumelty was his man.

'Scotland Yard was in touch with the American police about him both before and after his arrest' - just as they were in touch with the French, Austrian and Portuguese authorities on similar wild goose chases and with a similar lack of results.

Inspector Andrews 'was sent with other officers to pursue him to New York'. In fact, Walter Andrews was sent to Montreal, Canada, with two bank bombers, Roland Gideon and Israel Barnet. He was then directed to New York, but precisely why is unknown. Chief Inspector Thomas Byrne, one of New York's finest, interviewed by the American press, openly admitted to tailing Tumblety but he was cagey about why. The 'doctor' had of course just jumped bail, but the gross indecency charge was not one for which he could be extradited (murder was) so presumably, NYPD had their reasons for shadowing him. Even so, police suspicion does not make for incontrovertible proof.

The remaining four points from Evans and Gainey are weak in the extreme. Tumblety was wealthy enough to move around at will and to afford clothes to disguise himself. He was shrewd (!) and probably committed other offences elsewhere which are not known to be his. Several people in the States believed him to be Jack the Ripper.

So much for the 'case' against Tumblety. What of the objections? At fifty, he was at least fifteen years too old to fit any of the known Ripper sightings. At 5ft 10in he was too tall for any of the known Ripper sightings (and would have stood out like a sore thumb among the stunted derelicts of the Abyss). All known portraits of him show a ludicrously exaggerated sense of dress and a huge moustache. Only George Hutchinson's description comes anywhere near this and his man is plainly too short to be Tumblety.

The most damning case against Evans and Gainey's suspect however is his extraordinarily high profile. The man who kills women in a dingy backstreet is not a self-publicist. That is why we can now discard all the Ripper letters as hoaxes. Tumblety rode grey horses, strolled ostentatiously with a pair of greyhounds, wore bogus military uniform and claimed to walk with kings. If such a man had got away with five murders (and more elsewhere, as Evans and Gainey hint) he would have shouted about it from some non-extraditable roof tops a very safe distance from Scotland Yard. Instead, he complained bitterly about press defamation - 'how utterly base and wholly groundless these aspersions were.'

2

4) THE LOCALS

What if the Ripper wasn't an outsider of any kind? Whoever the killer was, he knew those mean streets like the back of his hand. No 'foreign skipper', no American quack, no 'mad Russian agent' was ever to command the expertise with which Jack eluded the patrols out to catch him. Who were they, these men who walked the Abyss?

a) William Bury

Bury belongs to the ranks of George Chapman and Neill Cream. Unlike most of the suspects in this book we know he was a killer. His story is every bit as bizarre as that of the Ripper murders themselves. Bury sold sawdust for a living and was married to a prostitute named Ellen Elliot, who seems to have been extraordinarily well off by the standards of her class and calling. The couple moved to Dundee, Scotland, in January 1889 and the following month Bury strangled Ellen with a rope, mutilated the body with a knife and forced it into a trunk. He then went to the local police with a concocted story that no one was likely to believe. He was hanged for her murder in April 1889.

   His links with the Ripper killings are remote. It has been suggested that he could have got to Whitechapel easily with his innocuous sawdust cart from Bow - which is true - and that he didn't kill in October because the month was foggy, which would hardly have dampened down the ardour of a serial killer. The theory goes that his wife suspected he was the Ripper - for which there is of course no evidence - and this accounts for his killing her. The use of the rope for strangulation is atypical of the Ripper killings; but above all is Bury's extraordinary stupidity in comparison with Jack's cunning. Whereas the Ripper vanished into the night virtually without trace, Bury went to the police (which he was obviously not bound to do) and told them that his wife had committed suicide! That alone makes Bury and Jack two very different men.

0

b) William Grainger

In March 1895, William Grainger slashed the abdomen of prostitute Alice Grahame on the Tenter Ground in Spitalfields. They had quarrelled, probably over the price of her services and the police picked him up. He served seven years of a ten year sentence. Grainger was an Irishman who had been dismissed from the Cork City Artillery for bad conduct. He seems to have wandered between Cork and London in the years 1887 to 1891 and was constantly being fleeced by the inhabitants of the Abyss. He may or may not have had medical training and worked as a fireman on a cattle boat at the time of his arrest.

An interesting possibility is that 'one person whom the police believe to have actually seen the Whitechapel murderer' was called in to identify Grainger at a police line-up and did so. If this was Joseph Lawende, who saw the Ripper in Mitre Square, his identification is likely to have been a figment of journalistic imagination. We know that Lawende saw his man briefly and said he would not know him again.

Even so, a knife attack on a prostitute in an area he seems to have known gives us a faint glimmer of a genuine suspect. What is inexplicable is why Grainger seems to have waited seven years between his attacks on Mary Kelly and on Alice Grahame.

0

c) James Kelly

Bury and Grainger had some claim to have been contemporary suspects, but James Kelly was not. By the time of the Ripper killings, he was already a convicted murderer, having disposed of his wife Sarah after an abscess in his neck caused serious mood swings. Kelly's death sentence was commuted and he was sent to Broadmoor from where he escaped in January 1888. Theorist John Morrison, who has erected a headstone over Mary Kelly's unmarked grave, believes that James Kelly killed his wife because of his affair with Mary. Having found out, however, that Mary was on the streets, he killed her and all the women from whom he had learned her whereabouts.

Again, we have the same problem we have met before. If Mary Kelly was the real target, why risk four other murders before reaching her? There is no actual evidence to link the Kellys at all. The most remarkable thing about James Kelly is that he was on the run from the asylum for thirty-nine years and only ended his days at Broadmoor because he voluntarily returned there in 1927!

0

d) Joseph Barnett

Two theorists, Bruce Paley and Paul Harrison, have hit upon the same potential Ripper in Joseph Barnett, the common law husband of Mary Kelly. Barnett was a Billingsgate fish porter, licensed in 1878 with his brothers, Daniel and Dennis. He met Mary Kelly in Commercial Street in April 1887 and lived with her until two weeks before she died. From July 1888 Barnett was unemployed, possibly having been dismissed for theft.

At the end of October, Barnett quarrelled with Mary, perhaps because she invited prostitute Julia van Turney to stay in the tiny room at Miller's Court. It is possible that the 'Danny' seen drinking with Mary in the Horn of Plenty on the night of her death was either Barnett's brother or even Barnett himself. On his own admission, he left Mary at Miller's Court at eight o'clock that night and went back to Buller's lodging house in Bishopsgate.

The police grilled Barnett for four hours and checked his clothes for bloodstains. He subsequently gave evidence at Mary Kelly's inquest and disappeared from history, dying in Shadwell in 1926.

Obviously anyone close to a murder victim is a suspect. 'Murder by person or persons unknown' is considerably rarer in the scheme of things than people think. When a wife is murdered, the police pay close attention to the husband. So it was with Joe Barnett. He fits in a general sense one of the eyewitness accounts of the Ripper, but his appearance, from the newspaper sketches of the time, is very nondescript. Bruce Paley puts forward the motive that Barnett killed the first four to frighten Mary off the streets (which seems a little draconian!) When this failed, he killed Mary herself, ripping her apart in his anger. This, Paley contends, is why the killings stopped - there was simply no need to continue.

He also maintains that Barnett fits the psychological profiling of the Ripper now available, but the motive itself does not. A serial killer is driven to murder by what the Germans call 'lustmorden'. He does not do it to make a point. Paley points to Barnett's peculiar speech patterns reported at the inquest - he repeated the last four words of anything said to him. This is known as echolalia today and I knew an old lady in her seventies with the same problem. I never took her for a serial killer, however! The point is that Barnett, like all the people of the Abyss who gave evidence at the inquests, was in the spotlight. A woman of whom he was clearly fond had just been butchered and he was asked questions by strangers far above his station in the full glare of the media of the day. Small wonder his speech patterns were odd.

0

*Severin Klosowski, known as George Chapman.
Abberline said when he was caught 'You've got
Jack the Ripper at last.'*

e) Severin Klosowski aka George Chapman

High on priority lists of possible Rippers today is Severin Klosowski, hanged at Wandsworth in April 1903 for the murder of his common law wife, Maud Marsh. It was clearly no flippant one-liner that led Inspector Abberline to say to Sergeant Godley, who arrested Klosowski, 'You've got Jack the Ripper at last'; Abberline actually came to believe that he was the Ripper. By that time, fifteen years after the Autumn of Terror, the trail had gone very cold and perhaps Abberline, coming to the end of his career as a European 'Pinkerton Man' and contemplating retirement to Bournemouth, had too much time on his hands.

Klosowski was born in 1865 (making him, at twenty-three, a little young for the eyewitness descriptions of the Ripper in 1888) in the town of Nagornak, Poland. The list of medical qualifications given by Messrs. Begg, Fido and Skinner probably exaggerate his surgical ability, because when he arrived in England in the spring or summer of 1887, he worked, not in a hospital, but as an assistant hairdresser in the West India Dock Road. By the time of the Ripper killings he was probably running his own hairdressing business in Cable Street in the parish of St George's-in-the-East. By 1890, he was working in a basement barber shop near George Yard.

Abberline's assertion that this places Klosowski near to the scene of the first murder is therefore wrong on two counts. Martha Tabram died in George Yard two years before Klosowski moved there and in any case, Martha Tabram was not murdered by Jack the Ripper!

In October 1889 Klosowski 'married' (there was no actual ceremony or civil contract) a Polish girl, Lucy Baderski and the son born to them, Vladislav, seems to have died within weeks. This may or may not have been the reason that Klosowski and his 'wife' emigrated to New Jersey in April 1891.

In Jersey City, the Klosowskis quarrelled, Severin going for Lucy with a knife and terrifying her so much that she came back without him in February 1892.

Klosowski followed soon after and met Annie Chapman (no relation to the Ripper victim), made her pregnant and lived with her for a while. From 1894 onwards, Klosowski used the name George Chapman exclusively, even though he had abandoned Annie and went on to take up with Mary Spink (whom he subsequently 'married' and murdered); Bessie Taylor (ditto) and Maud Marsh (ditto again). By this time (October 1902) the Marsh family doctor became suspicious of Maud's emaciated and exhausted state and had a post-mortem carried out. Her stomach, bowels, kidneys, liver and brain contained 7.24 grains of antimony, an irritant poison. The bodies of Mary Spink and Bessie Taylor were both exhumed and the tell-tale preserved skin, nails and hair showed that they too had died that way.

There is no doubt that Klosowski was guilty of the crime for which he was hanged, although his motive is tricky, in that he obtained no financial gain and, as there was no actual marriage, could have walked out on Mary, Bessie and Maud as he had on Annie Chapman. What is in serious doubt is Abberline's belief that he was the Whitechapel murderer.

Abberline told the *Pall Mall Gazette* in 1903 that 'there are a score of things which make one believe that Chapman is the man.' Among these, he cites: Klosowski's medical training, his arrival in London shortly before the murders began, his leaving so soon after they ended, the outbreak of a spate of murders in America while Klosowski was there and his knife attack on Lucy Baderski. Abberline also believed that Klosowski's appearance fitted various eyewitness accounts. Without the benefit of a century of research into serial killers' psyches, he glossed over Klosowski's apparent change of M.O. from sudden slash to periodic poison:

Detective Sergeant Godley was involved in the early stages of the Ripper case and achieved fame later as the man who arrested Severin Klosowski.

> You see, incentive changes; but the fiendishness is not eradicated. The victims . . . continue to be women; but they are of different classes and obviously call for different methods of dispatch.

Apart from showing his snobbery, Abberline was also displaying a profound ignorance of murder. How accurate are his 'score of things'?

First, his assertion that the Ripper murders began shortly after Klosowski's arrival in England. Even allowing for Abberline's contention that Martha Tabram was his first victim (she was murdered on August 7 1888) that means that at least fourteen months elapsed between the Pole's arrival and the 'first' killing.

Second, the ex-Inspector's view of Klosowski's medical skills. He was certainly apprenticed to a surgeon in Zvolen, Poland, but his actual work may have been confined to applying leeches and cups, which hardly makes him qualified to remove uteri and kidneys, at speed and in the dark.

Third, the spate of murders that occurred in America on Klosowski's arrival. In fact, 'spate' is rather a misnomer. In a single act of vicious violence, prostitute Carrie Brown, known as 'Old Shakespeare', was hacked to death in a hotel room on the Manhattan waterfront, New York on April 24, 1891.

'Choked, then mutilated,' screamed the *New York Times,* 'A Murder like one of Jack the Ripper's deeds. Whitechapel's horrors repeated in an East Side lodging house.'

The clue lies in the word 'repeated'. 'Old Shakespeare' may well have been the victim of a copycat killing (the actual Ripper murders were reported in detail in the American press) and a man answering the description of a foreigner seen with Carrie Brown shortly before she died might well have been the Algerian Arab Amir Ben Ali who was convicted of her murder, then released eleven years later. We know, as probably Abberline did not, that Klosowski was still in Whitechapel on February 5 1891. There is no record of his sailing to New York, yet we are expected to believe that the Pole was sufficiently au fait with the habits of East Side whores to kill Carrie in a city in which he did not live only days after arriving in America. Likewise, Abberline's assertion that the Ripper killings ended with Klosowski's emigration is patent nonsense. There were at least sixteen months between Mary Kelly's death and Klosowski's sailing. Only if we accept (as probably Abberline did) that the murder of 'Carrotty Nell' in Swallow Gardens, Whitechapel on February 13 1891 was also the work of the Ripper, does this contention make any sense. Klosowski's attack on Lucy Baderski has far more to do with East End violence generally than any Ripper specifics. The Pole was an undoubted womanizer and had a homicidal streak. The fact that he owned a knife hardly condemns him; he later threatened one 'wife' with a revolver and actually killed her with antimony. There is only one recorded serial killer in history who varied his weaponry to this extent.

The eyewitness accounts to which Abberline refers hold little water either. Witnesses like Israel Schwartz and Joseph Lawende referred to a little round sailors' cap. Klosowski certainly owned one of these, but so did vast numbers of the people of the Abyss. It was incidentally, common wear in both Eastern Europe and America at the time. Klosowski was known to be a flashy dresser - and this fits George Hutchinson's description of the man he saw with Mary Kelly, but the moustache was so ubiquitous in 1888 as to be an almost meaningless observation.

What Abberline presented to the *Gazette* in 1903 was an extremely flimsy circumstantial case which later researchers have demolished. What is extraordinary is the motive that the retired inspector ascribed to Klosowski. Referring to a rumour, current in the Autumn of Terror, that an American was offering up to £20 to buy uteri from the London medical schools (which actually fits Tumbelty better than Klosowski), Abberline believed 'some abandoned wretch' (i.e. Klosowski) may have been persuaded by that same American to obtain specimens for him from the unfortunates who wandered the Abyss. This was of course totally unnecessary. Specimens could be obtained for genuine medical purposes by anyone who cared to pose - as Tumbelty did - as a doctor. The idea that Klosowski was a hit-man who took colossal risks for a possible total of £100 (but an actual total of £40) defies belief.

He wrote his own memorial cards:

> Farewell, my friends, fond and dear,
> Weep not for me one single tear,
> For all that was and could be done,
> You plainly see my time has come.

2

5) THE POLICEMEN

It has now been some years since the late William Rushton spilled the beans in his *Reluctant Euro* that the villain in Agatha Christie's extraordinarily long-running West End play *The Mousetrap* is the policeman. For all those Ripperologists and historians who find it unbelievable that Jack could have escaped from such tight Whitechapel corners time after time, the notion of a police cover-up is tantalising.

a) Sir Robert Anderson - see under 'The Royals'

b) The Railway Policeman

In *Murder Most Foul*, the current true crime quarterly, theorist Bernard Brown of the Metropolitan Police has expanded on the fascinating idea he put forward in 1995 to the *Journal of Police History Society* - that the Ripper was able to come and go like a phantom because he disappeared in the swirling steam of the Underground ventilation shafts and used the Underground for a fast getaway.

The first 'tube' station in Whitechapel, that of the East London Railway, opened in 1876. Another, with stations there and at Mile End, opened in 1884. The Metropolitan, District, Great Eastern, South Eastern and South Coast companies all ran their trains through the area and they all had police units of their own. The terror of women travelling on trains had never quite disappeared and the murky corners and black tunnels of the Underground were a muggers' and rapists' paradise.

How close were the various stations to the Ripper killings? Shoreditch Station lay at the northern end of Brick Lane, less than five minutes away from Buck's Row; Whitechapel Station was even nearer. St Mary's Station, closed in 1938, stood on the south side of the Whitechapel Road, just yards from Berner Street.

Intriguingly, Brown believes it was tramway construction that caused the lull in the killings in October - and not the fog suggested in the case against William Bury. The new tramway meant that horse-drawn traffic was being rerouted through the tangled streets of the Abyss. More than that, Jack's targets - the whores of Whitechapel - were being kept unusually busy by the temporary influx of navvy labour. If Brown is right, then perhaps Jack couldn't quite wait. He killed Mary Kelly on November 9, whereas the tramway wasn't finished until the 15th.

Unfortunately, three things weaken Brown's case. The first is that he makes the wrong assumption that *all* the murders in the area between 1888 and 1892 were Jack's work - even the limbless torso found and never identified among the foundations of Norman Shaw's new opera house, soon to become New Scotland Yard. Secondly, he offers fascinating explanations for some of the 'clues' in the Ripper letters, such as:

> I have laughed when they look so clever and talk about being on the right track.

We now know that none of these letters is genuine.

The third weakness is that Brown does not put a name to his murderous copper. He does mention that two detectives on the case had experience as railway policemen - Inspector Richard Webb of J Division and Inspector Henry Moore at the Yard.

Without a name, we are not much further forward than the police were in 1888.

Certainly, a policeman in uniform would inspire a certain confidence in the wary. A 'boy in blue' might well lure anyone into an alley or a court before his real intentions became known. And it's even possible that one of the constables who gave evidence at the inquests is our man, his truncheon-pocket stuffed with a surgeon's knife, his foul-weather cape covering the blood on his gloves and greatcoat. But not one single eyewitness remembers any of the five victims talking to a policeman at any time on the night of their deaths, if we discount George Hutt at Bishopsgate station where Kate Eddowes spent some time sobering up.

Without tangible evidence of this sort, P.C. Jack must be dismissed.

0

6. THE OTHERS

When we start to look beyond the Abyss for Jack the Ripper, the chances of our being right diminish. Modern theories, clever indeed, ingenious - as some of them are, will generally tend to be less likely than contemporary ones.

a) Sir George Arthur

The English have been described as a lord-loving people. We even prefer our murderers to be 'toffs'. Arthur was in fact what the Victorians called a 'swell' - a wealthy man who slummed in poor areas - and he was in Whitechapel at the time of the Ripper murders. Such a pastime now would be regarded as hideously politically incorrect, but it was fashionable in Arthur's day. Even so, it was a risky business - a well dressed man in the traditional top hat and cape was himself an obvious target for street crime. Arthur wore a shooting coat and slouch hat.

At twenty-eight, he was exactly the right age for eyewitness accounts of the Ripper and his appearance could well have fitted the shabby genteel descriptions referred to by some. The Old Etonian was gazetted to the 2nd Life Guards in 1880 and went on to serve in Egypt and South Africa before writing a number of military biographies of Kitchener, Haig and Wolseley.

He was arrested on suspicion, but soon released.

0

b) Thomas Cutbush

The name Cutbush appears in the famous memoranda of Chief Constable Melville McNaghten in which he demolishes the case against this man after the *Sun* newspaper made allegations that he (Cutbush) was the Ripper. The claim was made in February 1894 and referred to a man who was already known to the police.

Thomas Hayne Cutbush was the nephew of a Scotland Yard Superintendent and lived well away from the Abyss in Albert

Street, Kennington. By 1888 he was in his early twenties and behaving oddly. He lost one job after another - sacked from a tea company in the Minories, then from door-to-door canvassing - and began to wander the streets at night. Exactly where he was when the famous five died we don't know.

He attacked Florence Johnson and Isabelle Anderson in Kennington with a knife he had bought in Houndsditch (on the edge of Ripper territory) stabbing both women from behind early in March 1891. He was apparently carrying out copycat attacks after a man named Colicott (his Christian name has not survived) who similarly stabbed six girls in their bustles in the same area weeks before. Colicott was arrested but had to be released because of faulty identification.

Cutbush was charged with malicious wounding having been arrested by Inspector William Race and sent to Broadmoor where he died in 1903.

The suggestion was that Cutbush was suffering from delusions brought on by tertiary syphilis, but the fact that his uncle the Superintendent blew his brains out in front of his own daughter in 1896 after years of depression and similar delusions, implies an hereditary problem in the Cutbush family. The knife that Cutbush used bore no resemblance to the likely murder weapon in the Ripper case.

0

c) Frederick Deeming

'Mad Fred' came from a family whose hold on reality seems to have been slight. His father died 'an imbecile' in a Birkenhead workhouse, having tried to commit suicide four times by cutting his throat. Frederick, the youngest of seven children, born in 1852, became an adventurer in his teens and travelled in the South African goldfields in the days of Cecil Rhodes. When his travels took him to Calcutta, India, he had what his family described as a 'severe attack of brain-fever' and suffered from delusions after that. He wore the crape weepers of an undertaker and said that his dead mother appeared to him regularly. In 1890 he was in Antwerp calling himself Lord Dunn.

A year later he moved into Dinham Villa, Rainhill, between St Helens and Liverpool, and, posing as a single man (he was by now married with four children), began a courtship of Emily Mather, the daughter of the Villa's owner. Then his inconvenient family turned up.

Deeming killed all five of them - Maria and their four children - by crushing their skulls with a blunt instrument and buried them

Frederick Bailey Deeming, who did his best to destroy two families, one in Britain, one in Australia. His 'confession' to the Ripper killings seems never to have happened.

in the new cement floors he laid himself at the Villa. Announcing that his 'sister' and her children had suddenly left, he married Emily Mather and the newly weds set sail for Australia, arriving in Melbourne in December 1891.

Here, Mr and Mrs 'Williams' rented a house in Andrew Street, Windsor and before Christmas, the newly laid cement floor had a single female occupant. Although the authors of *Jack the Ripper A-Z* refer to Deeming as a plumber and fitter, his DIY this time was sloppy. The house's owner dug up the badly laid floor and found the trussed up body of Emily Deeming, her skull shattered, her throat cut.

Deeming was eventually traced in Perth in March 1892 and stood trial the following month back in Melbourne on a charge of murder. He feigned insanity, though he probably was genuinely syphilitic and denounced women in general as the spreaders of disease. The corpses of his first family were dug up at Rainhill during the course of the trial and it took the jury less than an hour to find him guilty.

While awaiting execution in Melbourne jail, Deeming confessed to the murders of Liz Stride and Kate Eddowes and he died, smoking a cigar and watched by 10,000 people, on May 23 1892. His head was modelled for a death mask which found its way to Scotland Yard's macabre Black Museum.

The *Melbourne Evening Standard* warmed to Deeming's confession - 'Jack the Ripper: Deeming at Aldgate on the night of the Whitechapel murders.'

Reliable information however places him in South Africa in the Autumn of Terror. Again, we have the dissimilarity of crime and M.O. At no time did the Ripper use a blunt instrument or batter the head; and the likelihood is that he killed strangers at random, not his 'wives'. Deeming's lawyer denied that the man had made any confessions at all.

0

d) M.J. Druitt

For many years, ever since the publication of McNaghten's Memoranda, the prime suspect in the Ripper case was Montague John Druitt. 'The truth,' wrote McNaghten with a sad knack for accurate prophecy, 'will never be known and did indeed, at one time lie at the bottom of the Thames . . .'

Montague John Druit in pensive mood. A barrister and teacher, fears that he was 'going to be like mother', who was insane, may have led to his suicide in the Thames shortly after the murder of Mary Kelly. His resemblance to the Duke of Clarence is striking and eyewitness accounts may well describe him.

Mr M.J. Druitt, a doctor of about 41 years of age and of fairly good family, who disappeared at the time of the Miller's Court murder and whose body was found floating in the Thames on 31st Dec. i.e. 7 weeks after the said murder. The body was said to have been in the water for a month or more - on it was found a season ticket between Blackheath and London. From private information I have little doubt but that his own family suspected this man of being the Whitechapel murderer; it was alleged that he was sexually insane.

Druitt was an appealing suspect because of McNaghten's theory, still credible today, that:

> a much more rational and workable theory . . . is that the 'ripper's' brain gave way altogether after his awful glut in Miller's Court and that he then committed suicide . . .

Montague Druitt was born in August 1857, which made him thirty-one at the time of the Ripper killings, not forty-one as McNaghten believed. He was educated at Winchester and New College, Oxford and although his third class degree was hardly spectacular, he graduated in classics, not medicine. At no time could he be described as a doctor. In 1880, he began teaching at a boys' boarding school in Eliot Place, Blackheath and, brilliant sportsman that he was, became heavily involved in local cricket and hockey clubs. In 1881 he turned to law, was admitted to the Inner Temple in 1882 and called to the Bar in 1885. Far from being the failed lawyer that is our traditional picture of him, he did well as a barrister and was a special pleader for the Western Circuit. He seems to have kept on the teaching job as a second string and was well off by 1888.

It was then that things began to go wrong for him. His father had died three years earlier and this may have unhinged his mother who was sent to the Brooke Asylum in Clapton in July. On or about November 30 he was dismissed from the school by the headmaster, George Valentine, and the return ticket found in his pocket a month later when he was fished out of the Thames indicates that he threw himself in, probably at Hammersmith, on Saturday December 1st.

The body was found by waterman Henry Winslade off Thorneycroft's Wharf, Chiswick on the last day of 1888. He was fully clothed, had £2 17s 2d in cash, two cheques (which may have been his severance pay from the Blackheath school), a silver watch, a pair of gloves and a handkerchief, apart from the railway ticket already mentioned. There were four large stones in his overcoat pockets.

At the inquest, the coroner read the tragic letter found among Druitt's papers - 'Since Friday [presumably the day of his dismissal] I felt I was going to be like mother and the best thing for me was to die.'

There was a history of depression in the Druitt family - Montague's mother attempted suicide, and an aunt and older sister had succeeded.

Philip Sugden says that the view that Druitt was dismissed for molestation of one or more of his pupils is mere conjecture and anyway, he still had his lucrative law practice. He has missed the point that public schools like Winchester, and quite possibly the boarding establishment at Eliot Place, Blackheath, were hotbeds of homosexual activity. No researcher has produced a woman in Druitt's life, popular, handsome and successful though he appeared to be. Bearing in mind the new homophobia of the times - Henry Labouchere's bill had been recently passed, the scandals of the male brothel at Cleveland Street and of Oscar Wilde were soon to break - if that was the cause of Druitt's dismissal, he could also kiss goodbye to his law practice.

None of this, of course, except perhaps McNaghten's veiled 'it was alleged that he was sexually insane', has any bearing on the Ripper case. Journalist Daniel Farson, writing in 1959, became convinced that the case against Druitt could be found in a pamphlet called *The East End Murderer - I Knew Him*, printed privately in the Dandenong, Australia. This document briefly passed through Farson's hands but it was stolen before he could check it. He believed however - and attempted to verify it by travelling to Australia in search of Mr Fell, the printer - that the author was Dr Lionel Druitt, Montague's cousin, who briefly shared with Dr Thynne a surgery at Number 140, The Minories. If Montague visited the surgery, watched cousin Lionel at work, 'borrowed' a knife, then he was within a short walk of the Abyss and had a bolt-hole to run to when the police patrols began to multiply.

In fact, it is not possible to verify any of this. There is no *established* link between Druitt and the Whitechapel area, no link at all with knives or violence. He may have been homosexual, but that did not give him a hatred of whores. The problem is that McNaghten was voicing his theories on evidence which no longer exists - 'from private information . . .' - and we have no means now of knowing what he meant. His knowledge of Druitt, bearing in mind he claims to have heard it all from one of the man's own family, is woefully inaccurate. He gets his age wrong, his occupation wrong, the date of his suicide wrong. If Druitt was the Ripper, he was still walking around London three weeks after he butchered Mary Kelly, and apparently, until Friday November 30,

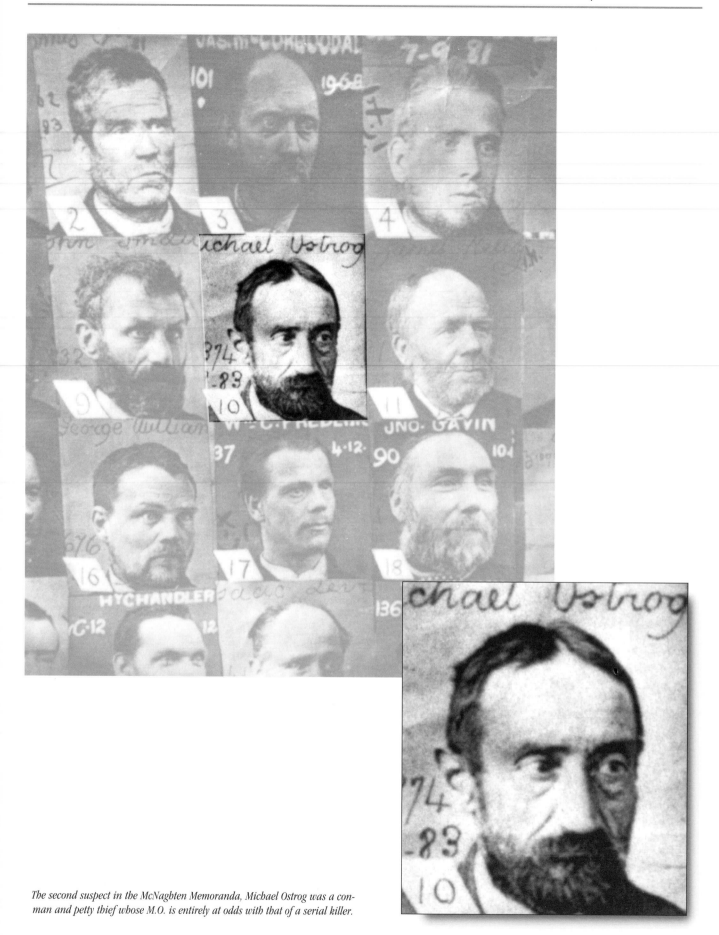

The second suspect in the McNaghten Memoranda, Michael Ostrog was a con-man and petty thief whose M.O. is entirely at odds with that of a serial killer.

behaving perfectly normally. Apart from the lack of evidence against Druitt, the most compelling thing in his favour is that he very nearly has alibis for the times of at least two of the murders. For instance, Annie Chapman died between five and six o'clock on the morning of September 8. Five hours later, Druitt was coolly batting against the Brothers Christopherson at Blackheath. A week earlier, when Polly Nichols met Jack, Druitt was knocking them for six at Canford, Dorset, miles away from the murder scene and less than six hours later.

And Abberline's comment on Druitt?

> Yes, I know all about that story . . . but there is absolutely nothing beyond the fact that he was found at the time [in the Thames] to incriminate him.

0

e) Michael Ostrog

The third of Melville McNaghten's suspects from his Memoranda is, in many ways, the most bizarre of all.

> Michael Ostrog, a mad Russian doctor and a convict and unquestionably a homicidal maniac. This man was said to have been habitually cruel to women and for a long time was known to have carried about with him surgical knives and other instruments; his antecedents were of the very worst and his whereabouts at the time of the Whitechapel murders could never be satisfactorily accounted for.

Mixing homicidal mania with being Russian *and* a doctor, Ostrog looks almost too good to be true. And indeed, he is! Philip Sugden has researched the man in detail, providing information about a character of whom almost nothing was known and proving McNaghten, once again, wrong on almost every count.

Ostrog was certainly a criminal. The long list of fraud, deception and theft for which he was convicted leaves no doubt of that, but he also emerges as rather inept and, dare I say it, rather cute! He was *probably* Russian and Ostrog is *probably* his real name although he told so many lies that nothing is certain. He was born about 1833, making him *far* too old for any of the eyewitness sightings of Jack in Whitechapel. He used a number of aliases in a life of crime that spanned over a quarter of a century up to 1888. He was often Max Sobieski, a dispossessed Polish nobleman; he was sometimes Dr Grant or Dr Bonge, a distinguished medico; occasionally he was Bertrand Ashley, Ashley Nabokoff, or Claude Clayton. He was a Russian naval surgeon, a student who had fled Heidelberg to avoid fighting a duel. Occasionally, he claimed to have killed a man in a duel. Now and then, certainly when visiting the breweries of Burton-on-Trent, he was a Swede.

He targeted the soft touches - Eton schoolboys (on a weekend when by an extraordinary coincidence, Melville McNaghten was playing against the First Eleven of his old school); Oxford and Cambridge undergraduates (who had a good deal more money then than they have today) and benign old clergymen. He stole jewellery, silver cups, books, told hard-luck stories of being pursued by the vengeful and appalling Russian police just because he was a Pole, and wined and dined wherever he could at somebody else's expense.

We know from police records that he was nearly five feet eleven tall - far too tall for any of the eyewitness accounts of Jack - and had scars on his back from flogging. Only once did he display any violence - he waved a revolver at Superintendent Oswald or Oswell at Burton, before turning it, rather halfheartedly, on himself.

In September 1887 Ostrog was sentenced at the Old Bailey, and displayed signs of insanity which the police believed were faked. At the end of the month he was transferred to the Surrey Pauper Lunatic Asylum from which he was released in March 1888. His exact whereabouts at the time of the Ripper murders are, as McNaghten says, unknown, but it is likely he was in Paris (which certainly eliminates him) where he was sentenced to two years for theft on November 18. There he used the name Stanistan Sublinsky. Ostrog was last heard of, partially crippled, in the St Giles Christian Mission in Holborn in 1904.

Why does Melville McNaghten suggest this man? Undoubtedly because of pressure from Dr Forbes Winslow and the howling, hysterical press, the City Force, if not the Met, were actually checking asylums to see if any recently released or escaped inmates might fit Jack's bill. Whether Ostrog was real or faking, the *Police Gazette* of October 26 1888 described him as being wanted by the police (he was a 'ticket-of-leave man' on parole and had failed to report to them) saying 'special attention is called to this dangerous man'.

McNaghten is certainly right when he refers to Ostrog's 'antecedents' (criminal record), but there is no evidence whatsoever of cruelty to women (on the contrary, he was polite and courteous to everyone) nor in the fact that he habitually carried knives with him. Again, the CID man seems to be relying on hearsay. He wrote his Memoranda while Ostrog was still alive, but showed no inclination, as far as is known, to interview him or take the inquiries any further.

0

f) Robert Stephenson

Victorian society seems to abound with oddballs. The big difference between then and now is that there were more gentlemen per head of the population with time on their hands and more money relative to the rest of society to indulge themselves. Such a one was the theorist-turned-suspect Robert Donston Stephenson, who usually called himself Dr Roslyn D'Onston.

He was born in April 1841, the son of a seed-oil mill owner from Hull, and became obsessed with magic as a child. In 1859, having studied chemistry and medicine at Munich and Paris universities, he met Sir Edward Bulwer-Lytton:

Robert Donston Stephenson called himself Roslyn D'Onston and was a self-publicist and Black Magician. His assertions are unverifiable and should be taken with an enormous pinch of salt.

'the great Magist', the one man in modern times for whom all systems of ancient and modern magism and magic, white or black, held back no secrets.

He learned at the master's knee.

The Order of the Golden Dawn, to which Dr William Wynn Westcott belonged, was considered tame stuff by the pretentious and peculiar factory owner's son from Hull. He joined Garibaldi's army of Red Shirts fighting for Italian unification and moved to London where he wrote freelance articles for the *Pall Mall Gazette.* His behaviour by 1887-8 was certainly anti-social. A police inspector, Thomas Roots, who had known him since the 1860s, described him as a drinker and drug-user and certainly the use of narcotics was not only linked with 19th century occultism, but may explain Stephenson's irrational and cryptic behaviour. A Robert Stephenson was charged with assault at Thames Magistrates' Court in June 1887 and indecent assault on October 30 1888. His biographer, Melvyn Harris, hints that the dismembered woman found floating in the Thames at Rainham, Essex and in the St Mary's Lock, Regent's Canal were Stephenson's first experiments in ritual murder - the bits were the last mortal remains of Stephenson's wife.

In July 1888 he booked himself into the London Hospital, complaining of tension and sleeplessness and stayed there for

134 days, writing to inform the City of London police on October 16 that the spelling of 'Juwes' in the Goulston Street scribblings was really 'Juives' - in other words, the Ripper was a Frenchman. On December 1 he wrote an article on the case for the *Pall Mall Gazette.*

The case against Stephenson is flimsy. He was in the area at the time certainly (along with nearly half a million inhabitants of the Abyss) but the thought of his return after his slashing forays to a *hospital* as his hiding place seems highly improbable. One of his acquaintances, Baroness Vittoria Cremers, told journalists in the 1920s that she found blood-encrusted ties in a box in Stephenson's room. Stephenson had told her that the Ripper had slipped the uteri and kidneys he stole under his tie to avoid detection. Even allowing for the width of ties in 1888, the mess this would cause would alert anyone passing Stephenson on the street on his way back to the London Hospital refuge.

Above all, Stephenson so shrouded himself in superstition and mumbo-jumbo that nothing we get from his writings or those of his Theosophist friends can be taken at face value.

0

James Maybrick, the Liverpudlian businessman murdered by his wife whose 'diary' inexplicably causes interest, despite its being exposed as a hoax.

g) James Maybrick

James Maybrick must be unique among Ripper suspects because he himself was the victim of murder. Born in 1839, Maybrick was a cotton-broker from Liverpool whose business brought him into contact with Americans. His wife, whom he married in 1881, was thirty-six year old Florence Elizabeth Chandler, a southern belle whose mother had been married three times. The rather dour Maybrick family disapproved of the marriage and in many ways the hypochondriac James, constantly using arsenic for aphrodisiac purposes, was not the ideal catch.

After three years in the States, the Maybricks moved into the impressive Battlecrease House, Aigburth, Liverpool with their two children, five servants and a nanny.

By 1887, the Maybrick marriage was decidedly rocky. He had a mistress, she had a lover (Alfred Brierley, one of Maybrick's friends) and the business was not going well. In keeping with thousands of men of all classes in Victorian Britain, Maybrick took to beating his wife.

On April 28, 1889, five months after the last of the Ripper killings, James Maybrick was taken ill. He died on May 11 after what seemed a slight recovery. Suspicion fell on 'Florrie' after her brothers-in-law found a packet in her room labelled 'Arsenic:

Poison for Cats'. It transpired that she had bought this and arsenic-soaked flypapers at a local chemist days before her husband changed his will. The new one did not mention Florrie at all.

The post-mortem revealed traces of arsenic, with its distinctive preservative qualities, in James Maybrick's body.

Florrie stood trial in July 1889. The judge in the case was Sir James Stephen (whose own son is now a Ripper suspect) who was losing his grip on reality prior to being sent to an asylum and who failed to direct the jury properly. What actually found Florence Maybrick guilty was the sexual prejudice of the day. Whereas James Maybrick's adultery merely gave Florrie a motive, her adultery was seen as all the more wicked and unforgivable and it was this bigotry that led to the death sentence. This was commuted and in 1904, having served fifteen years, she returned to America, dying at the age of seventy-six in 1941.

Why is James Maybrick linked with the Ripper killings? The sole evidence is the sixty-three page journal with the black and gold binding which alleges that Maybrick himself was the monster of the Abyss. The world of publishing is far less gullible than it used to be. The *Times* newspaper's purchase of the so-called Hitler Diaries led to a lot of egg on a lot of faces and various experts were called in to test the journal for authenticity. The book was given by Tony Devereux to his friend, scrap metal dealer Michael Barrett in 1991 and eventually found its way into print as *The Diary of Jack the Ripper* in 1993.

By the time the book hit the shelves - 'the day the world's greatest murder mystery will be solved' according to its hype - serious doubts had crept in. Chemical analysis of the ink used on what was undoubtedly a genuine Victorian scrapbook produced the likely result that it was a forgery, produced within twelve years either side of 1921. More recent work has moved these goalposts much nearer to our time, perhaps to the late 1980s, when Dr Bond's post-mortem report on Mary Kelly was found. The consensus of expert opinion on the style of writing is that huge clumps of the individual diary entries were probably written together and the formation of letters is not Victorian. It is inconceivable that any of the writing is Maybrick's hand, as his will and signature bear no comparison at all. Ripper expert Martin Fido has identified twenty examples of anachronisms in the text. The American publishing deal collapsed as a result of these doubts amid articles in the States with titles like 'Jack the Ripoff?' and Michael Barrett claimed via the Liverpool Daily Post in June 1994 to have forged the diary himself. His solicitors withdrew his confession the next day.

Within a short time of the journal's appearance, the Maybrick watch turned up opportunely to add veracity to the diary. The watch is undoubtedly Victorian, a gold pocket type made in Lancaster in 1846. Scratched onto the case are the words 'J. Maybrick', 'I am Jack' and the initials of the five victims - 'MN', 'AC', 'ES', 'CE' and 'MK'. Despite the fact that Dr Turgoose of UMIST (University of Manchester Institute of Science and Technology) found these scratchings compatible with the 1888 period using an electron microscope, I remain unimpressed. It is just too glib, knowing what we do about the journal.

One of the silliest arguments of all is the apparent letter 'M' daubed on the wall of 13 Miller's Court in Mary Kelly's blood. Theorist Shirley Harrison argues that this is an example of the killer's enormous ego and that the 'M' means Maybrick. Equally of course it could be 'M' for Mary or simply an accidental smear.

So what is dubious about the Maybrick journal? It claims that Maybrick wrote at least one of the letters. We know the real Ripper wrote none of them. It claims that the murderer left two coins at the feet of Annie Chapman. The Ripper left nothing. It claims that Mary Kelly's breasts were displayed on her bedside table. They weren't. It goes without saying that the real killer would have been able to distinguish between what he actually did and what subsequent reporters of his day and theorists since have invented or conjectured.

Philip Sugden wrote:

> A reading of the diary still leaves me baffled as to how any intelligent and reasonably informed student of the Ripper case could possibly have taken it seriously.

Bravo! Unfortunately, Ripperologist Melvyn Harris is also right when he notes that the Maybrick diary's 'time-wasting stupidities will linger on to dog historians for years to come.'

0

7) THE ROYALS

We are obsessed with homicidal monarchs. The 'real' Richard III is quite boring in contrast with the hunchbacked monster and murderer of eleven people created by Shakespeare. And what made it all the more fascinating to theatre-goers until 20th century research put them right is that it was supposedly all based on fact. The chroniclers Hall and Holinshed and worthy, even saintly men like Thomas More wrote it all down as history.

And there is something faintly appealing about Queen Victoria, all four feet ten of her, slashing and hacking her way through the East End. I must admit that when I first read the 'highest in the land' theory over twenty years ago, this is the abiding image I got - and the actual theories are no less ludicrous.

Let's look at the peripheral figures first before launching into the two brilliant, but impossible, theories that have grabbed the headlines over the last quarter century. The reason that the Royals have been put in the frame at all is that theorists reasoned there had to be an explanation for Jack not being caught. The explanation, they concluded, was that he was, which accounts for the sudden end to the killings after Mary Kelly. And because 'the highest in the land' was involved, there was the cover-up to end all cover-ups (at least until the Kennedy assassination!).

a) Leopold II, King of the Belgians

A member of the Saxe-Coburg family who inherited the throne of Belgium on the death of his father in 1865, Leopold was typical of a prince of his day: army officer, traveller and man-about-town. He was perhaps less typical in the personal, certainly callous and possibly unhealthy, interest he took in the African inhabitants of the Belgian Congo, which was his personal property until he handed it over to Belgium in 1908. Certainly, his private life had more than a whiff of scandal and he took two of his daughters to court over the fortune their mother had left them.

Everything else is speculation. Leopold had a house in England which Ripper researcher Jacquemine Charrot-Ludwidge believes was the house described by Robert Lees, the shadowy medium who claimed he helped the police with their enquiries. The theory goes that the atrocities Leopold witnessed in Africa turned an already unpleasant mind and that he made secret visits to London in the Autumn of Terror.

0

'Eddie' - the Duke of Clarence and Avondale - in the full dress uniform of a lieutenant of the 10th Prince of Wales's Own Hussars. His long neck required special tailoring and led to his nickname - 'Collars and Cuffs'.

b) Albert Victor, Duke of Clarence aka 'Eddie', 'Collar and Cuffs'

The monarchy in the 20th century might have gone in a very different direction if the eldest grandson of Victoria had lived to inherit his grandmother's vast Empire. It is highly likely that there would have been a Regency crisis at the very least and that possibly we would now be living in a republic.

'Eddie', as the family knew him, was the eldest son of 'Bertie', the Prince of Wales and his long-suffering wife, the Danish Princess Alexandra. He was born in 1864 and it soon became apparent that he suffered seriously from the same deafness that afflicted his mother. His speech patterns were unclear, his mouth hung open and his head tilted to one side in his attempts to understand what was being said to him. As a young man, his collars were cut high and stiff to prevent this tendency in public.

As heir presumptive he had duties and affairs of state which could not be avoided. He attended Trinity College, Cambridge, the university so loved by his grandfather, Prince Albert, in 1883, although very little study was possible for him. Nevertheless, in common with the sycophancy of the time, he was given an honorary Doctorate of Law in the same year the Ripper struck. He joined his father's regiment - the elite 10th Prince of Wales's Own Hussars - and became an unlikely Adjutant. Naïve paintings - very fashionable in his day - showed him mounted, in busby and plume, with the legend 'The Pet of the Tenth' inscribed below. He also joined his father's Masonic Lodge (his uncle, Arthur of Connaught, was the highest-ranking Mason in the land). In 1889 he became ADC to the Queen and took the title Duke of Clarence and Avondale in 1891. In December of that year he became engaged to Princess May of Teck (the future redoubtable Queen Mary), but died in the flu epidemic that swept the country in January 1892. Or did he? And thereby hangs another tale.

The idea that the Ripper was Clarence probably dates from 1960 and belongs to Dr Thomas Stowell who called his suspect 'S' (itself causing all kinds of confusion). Stowell's theory is that, just as Leopold of the Belgians acquired 'lustmord' by witnessing atrocities, so did Clarence after watching deer being butchered after weekend shoots or torn apart by hounds. He also claimed that Clarence was suffering from tertiary syphilis and this combination so affected his mind that he killed the famous five before himself being imprisoned and dying of the disease in 1892. Stowell wrote an article along these lines in *The Criminologist* in 1970 but subsequently wrote to the *Times* in November of that year:

> I have at no time associated His Royal Highness, the late Duke of Clarence, with the Whitechapel murderer or suggested that the murderer was of royal blood.

American writer Frank Spiering produced *Prince Jack,* which fleshed out the story, in 1978, but had Clarence been a contemporary suspect, which he was not, he can be discounted for a number of reasons. Despite the elaborate tosh of journalist Stephen Knight, there is nothing to link Clarence with the Abyss. He showed no interest in social reform or poverty and never went to the East End. Although his swarthy appearance could be taken as 'foreign', he is again too tall for any known eyewitness sighting (oddly, his resemblance to M.J. Druitt is extraordinary). Above all, he has a reasonably watertight alibi for all the killings.

When Polly Nichols died on August 31st, the Prince was at Derby Lodge in Yorkshire, the guest of Viscount Downe. He was there from August 29th to September 7th. From there, he went straight to the cavalry barracks in York, the day before Annie Chapman was killed, and stayed there until September 10th. On the night of the 'double event', Clarence was staying with his grandmother at Abergeldie in Scotland. According to the Queen's famous diary, he had lunch with her - this was ten hours after he supposedly butchered Kate Eddowes in Mitre Square. At the time of Mary Kelly's murder, Clarence was staying at Sandringham, the family home in Norfolk, where he was until November 12.

Conspiracy theorists will of course contend that he *could* have slipped away from any or all of the above places and that if the royal family noticed, they merely covered up the fact and sent the royal physician, Sir William Gull, haring off to catch him, declare him insane (which he was not strictly qualified to do) and detain him until the syphilis took its inevitable course. The point is that the evidence simply isn't there and the motivation is thin in the extreme.

0

J.K. Stephen, Eddie's tutor, was never the same after a blow to the head.

c) James Stephen

If not the heir presumptive, how about his tutor? James Kenneth Stephen is no more a contemporary suspect than his student, emerging in 1972 as a more likely suspect than Clarence. Born in 1859 (thus making him the 'right' age according to witnesses who saw Jack), he was a gifted intellectual with a public school and university background, graduating from Cambridge in 1882. The following year he acted as tutor to the Prince and became a Fellow of King's College in 1885.

In the winter of 1886-7 Stephen visited Felixstowe on the Suffolk coast and, while examining a pumping mill, was hit on the head by its revolving sails. The injury seemed minor enough, but it may have triggered problems which led to his subsequent insanity. Stephen's father, the judge at the Maybrick trial, also went insane and he himself had always exhibited signs of manic depression.

His literary output doesn't seem to have declined, as we might expect from a cousin of Virginia Woolfe. A frequent contributor to university journals, he wrote for the *Pall Mall Gazette* and published a pamphlet in defence of compulsory Greek the year before he died. Only a hundred years later would we detect signs of insanity in that! Michael Harrison, who proposed Stephen as a possible Ripper, found signs of misogyny and sadism in the man's poetry, providing a motive for being 'down on whores'.

> If all the harm that women have done
> Were put in a bottle and rolled into one,
> Earth would not hold it,
> The sky could not enfold it . . .

Harrison's theory goes that Stephen and Clarence were lovers at Cambridge (which is possible) and that when the affair ended, because of Clarence's position and the pressure of affairs of state, Stephen became unhinged. The murder dates to Harrison are significant because they would have meant something to Clarence in the intimate world in which they both moved.

Although more recent writers have plumped for Stephen, working in league with 'Prince Jack' and even with M.J. Druitt, the claim has no basis in fact. If we discount Clarence, as we must, we must also acquit poor J.K. Stephen who died, according to the medical report, at 4.21 p.m. on February 31 1892 of 'mania, refusal of food, exhaustion' at St Andrew's Hospital, Northampton.

0

d) Two Jacks and a Knave

When Stephen Knight died in 1985, speculation was rife. As well as pointing to a Masonic connection in the Ripper case in what is undoubtedly the most elaborate theory so far, he attacked Freemasonry head on in *The Brotherhood,* which appeared two years before he died. Eyebrows were raised. Knight was only thirty-three. The highest Masons in the land were those of the 33rd degree. The Masons had got him.

In fact he died from a cerebral tumour despite surgery, having developed epilepsy in 1977. Like the idea of a Masonic murder, his book has now been utterly discredited.

The story is highly complicated and was told to Knight by Joseph Sickert, who claimed to be son of Walter, a painter of some note, fleshed out by the research that Knight himself undertook. When the book first appeared, I was asked to deliver a lecture on the latest theory and I still have my annotated copy from that time. The whole tone of *The Final Solution* is one of shifting ground. Knight begins with speculation and query and ends up with 'proven fact'. In the process he distorts British history and supposes a great deal. And he gives the game away on almost every page. Walter Sickert, from whom the story supposedly emanated originally, was a 'renowned raconteur'. The story, as told by Joseph Sickert 'all sounded terribly unlikely'. Sickert himself was 'vague' and 'disordered'.

Walter Sickert at the time of the Ripper killings. He was the focus for the fascinating, if improbable, theories of Stephen Knight.

Alice Crook, the flower girl who fell for a prince - or did she?

The Prime Minister in 1888 was Robert Cecil, the Marquess of Salisbury. According to Stephen Knight, he was given task of covering up the scandal of the Queen's grandson's illicit marriage.

The story goes that Walter Sickert worked out of a studio in Cleveland Street, for which there is no actual evidence, and that across the road a Catholic girl called Annie Crook worked in a flower shop. As the Duke of Clarence was an occasional visitor to the homosexual brothel in Cleveland Street, raided by the police amid sensational scandal in 1889, he met and fell in love with Annie and subsequently married her. There is no evidence that Clarence ever visited this brothel, although various members of the aristocracy and senior officers of cavalry certainly did. The morganatic marriage is unrecorded and dates and names do not match up. Hovering over all Knight's thesis is the completely erroneous view that the royals were hideously unpopular, that England was on the brink of an anarchist revolution and that such a marriage was important anyway. Constitutionally, Clarence could not have married Annie Crook, simply because she was Catholic, so the subsequent bloody cover up was wholly unnecessary.

The witness at the clandestine marriage, the Sickerts go on, was Mary Kelly, and she saw the perfect opportunity to blackmail the government. The Prime Minister at the time was Robert Cecil, the Marquess of Salisbury, who, as a leading Freemason, consulted with fellow Lodge member and physician-in-ordinary to the Queen, Sir William Gull.

Gull set about the business of silencing Mary Kelly with surgical precision, leaving Masonic mementoes at the scene of the crime.

Sir William Withey Gull was Knight's Ripper, although the stroke he had suffered by the autumn of 1888 makes this highly unlikely.

John Netley was the coachman who took Gull on his Whitechapel wanderings. He also - according to Stephen Knight - tried to kill Annie Crook twice.

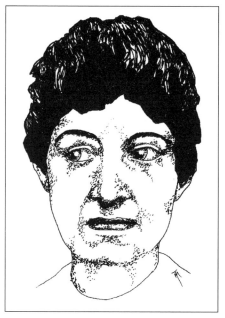

Annie Elizabeth Crook, the daughter of Eddie and Alice, bears a superficial resemblance to Eddie's mother, Princess Alexandra.

Unfortunately, an eminent surgeon could not know what the woman looked like or precisely where she lived and this is where Walter Sickert came in. It was this difficulty in hunting for Mary Kelly that led to Kate Eddowes' murder, in that she occasionally used 'Mary Kelly' as an alias in the Abyss. The others died because, as the real Mary Kelly's friends, they shared the secret of the clandestine marriage.

The reason, Knight claims, that the Ripper was never caught is that he was not one man, but three. Sickert kept watch (although for much of the book Knight suggests that Dr Robert Anderson of Scotland Yard obligingly fulfilled this role) and the murders themselves were either carried out in a carriage or the bloodstained Gull was whisked away in one. Other recent writers have supported the idea, saying that eyewitnesses would not have noticed a vehicle in the area. This shows no understanding of the Abyss at all. We have already seen how rare horsedrawn cabs of any kind were east of the Minories. Had the Ripper used one, *someone* would have commented.

The driver, say Sickert and Knight, was John Netley, a carman from Paddington who was killed in 1903 when his van hit a bollard near Baker Street. Netley was thrown out and his own van wheel smashed his head. According to Knight, Netley had often driven Clarence and Annie Crook to the Cleveland Street love nest. Not only that, he was a womanizer and opportunist, not averse to murder if the price was right. The child supposedly born to Clarence and Annie was Alice Margaret and Netley was employed to kill her too, so that no traces of the marriage survived. In 1888 and again in 1892 he drove his cab at the little girl, but missed both times. Netley's name appears in the pages of the so-called Abberline diaries.

With the obvious Masonic involvement, the 'clues' left behind suddenly fall into place. Newspaper accounts of the time suggest that a neat row of coins was found placed between Annie Chapman's feet and this, says Knight, is a Masonic symbol. The cutting of the throat, the ripping out of entrails and placing them over the left shoulder, even the choice of Kate Eddowes' murder site in Mitre Square, all have Masonic significance. Most dramatic of all however is the spelling of 'Juwes' on the wall of the Wentworth buildings, Goulston Street. This is not simply a misspelling of 'Jews', Knight argues, but refers to Jubela, Jubelo and Jubelum, the mythical apprentice Masons who murdered their master Hiram Abiff, who was working on the building of Solomon's Temple. These three were caught making their escape and put to death - 'by the breast being torn open and the heart and vitals taken out and thrown over the left shoulder'. Even the triangular flaps of skin on Kate Eddowes' cheeks are, says Knight, Masonic symbols.

What happened to the Rippers? According to the Sickert-Knight version, Gull died, hopelessly insane at some unspecified date. The 'funeral' which took place at Thorpe-le-Soken, Essex, was bogus - the coffin contained somebody else's body. John Netley, having failed for the second time to run over Alice Crook in 1892, was chased by a mob from Drury Lane to Westminster Pier, where he threw himself into the Thames and drowned. Waiter Sickert, paid £500 'hush money' by Salisbury, spent the best part of the rest of his life in Dieppe, a tortured, haunted soul, working cryptic clues to the Ripper murders into his paintings.

The only problem with the Sickert-Knight story is to know where to start to demolish it. Knight himself clearly was obsessed with Freemasonry and saw examples of its 'evils' everywhere. The 'Juwes' story, firmly rooted in legend, can be dismissed. So can Clarence's links with the Abyss. In his eagerness to find evidence, Knight frequently ignored dates and names in his records and has even been accused recently of making much of it up himself. Sir William Withey Gull had suffered two strokes by the Autumn of Terror and it is unlikely that he had the strength to carry out the mutilations Jack did. He died in 1890 after further strokes and there is no evidence to suggest a sham funeral at all. As we have seen, John Netley was killed in a road accident eleven years after Knight says he flung himself into the Thames. And it takes an *awful* lot of imagination to see anything to do with the Ripper in Walter Sickert's paintings.

The Abberline diaries, in which Netley's name appears, were not used by Stephen Knight and only came to light after his death. They are forgeries.

Undoubtedly clever though the theory is, the motivation in the Sickert-Knight story is weak in the extreme. Salisbury was not a Freemason, so why employ Gull? Assuming that the clandestine marriage was true (which it wasn't) why not simply buy the silence of Mary Kelly and co? Her Britannic Majesty's government could easily afford the paltry sums that they would ask for.

0

e) The Candlestick Maker

Theorist Melvyn Fairclough, a furniture restorer and friend of Joseph Sickert, took up in a sense where Stephen Knight left off. His work hinges on the diaries supposedly written by Inspector Abberline between his retirement in 1892 and 1915. No scientific analysis of these has been carried out à la the Maybrick journal, but details about Jack's victims seem to have been taken from a modern piece of research, complete with minor errors. Since his book *The Ripper and the Royals* was published in 1991, Fairclough has stated that he now believes the diaries are not genuine.

Because he was working with Joseph Sickert, the story in Fairclough's version follows the familiar line of the clandestine marriage, but it throws out two fascinating scenarios which are every bit as gripping as Stephen Knight's.

In Knight's version, the actual Ripper was William Gull, and Fairclough goes along with this. He is interested in bigger fish however and points to the instigators of the murders as members of the Royal Alpha Lodge No. 16, whose members were almost exclusively members of the aristocracy. Charles Warren was also a Mason, albeit not of the exalted company: so that his co-operation in the cover-up (for example his removal of the 'Juwes' scribblings) was assured. With the masonic conspiracy and obsession as a backdrop, anything is possible, so Fairclough trots out the poisoned grape theory and the killings in the coach. The fact that Dr William Sanders, the City of London analyst, found no trace of drugs in Kate Eddowes' stomach becomes irrelevant once Fairclough tells us that Sanders was a Mason.

The evidence that Fairclough uses to indicate that several of the victims were dumped where they were found is forensically unconvincing.

Joseph Sickert finally told Fairclough the name of the mastermind behind the killings, who had actually ventured into the Abyss himself to make sure the matter was being handled properly - Lord Randolph Churchill, called in the

Lord Randolph Churchill - the Candlestick Maker - whose general appearance conforms well with George Hutchinson's description of the Ripper (see page 85).

Abberline Diaries the 'Candlestick Maker'. As the senior Mason in the country, this was all part of Churchill's duty. The odd thing is that George Hutchinson's extraordinarily detailed description of the man he saw with Mary Kelly on the night of her death does bear a close resemblance to the flamboyant Lord Randolph. And as in the case of the mysterious doctor whose son died from venereal disease caught from a prostitute, Churchill was to die of syphilis in 1895. He was effectively out of things by 1888, having quarrelled with the Prince of Wales and the Prime Minister on two separate issues. It was typical of Churchill's bravado that he effectively destroyed himself by his own folly.

Melvyn Fairclough has picked up a minor piece of evidence, which at the time was dismissed as a mistake. Caroline Maxwell was the wife of Henry Maxwell, a lodging house deputy of Dorset Street. She had known Mary Kelly for four months and at the inquest, said:

> I was on speaking terms with her although I had not seen her for three weeks until Friday morning 9th instant about half past 8 o'clock She was standing at the corner of Miller's court in Dorset Street. I said to her, 'What brings you up so early' She said, 'I have the horrors of drink upon me as I have been drinking for some days past.' I said, 'Why don't you go to Mrs Ringer's [The Britannia] and have a half pint of beer?' She said, 'I have been there and had it, but I brought it all up again.' At the same time she pointed to some vomit in the roadway . . .

Mrs Maxwell said she saw Mary again about an hour later, standing outside The Britannia in the company of a market porter of medium height. She wore 'a dark dress, black velvet body and coloured wrapper round her neck.

Most theorists have rejected Caroline Maxwell's testimony - as did the coroner at the time - as a case of the wrong day, but Fairclough believes that she was right, and that the battered corpse in Number 13 Miller's Court was not Mary Kelly at all, but Winifred Collis, a friend of hers involved in the Cleveland Street goings on. The cry of 'Oh, murder!' (which I find equally false) was, says Fairclough, Mary Kelly discovering Winifred's body as she returned home at four in the morning. She then wandered around in shock until Caroline Maxwell saw her four hours later. With her face destroyed, says Fairclough, it wouldn't have been possible for Joseph Barnett to have identified Mary definitely. He makes the assumption that Mary's hair was a dark auburn - hence her nickname 'Ginger' - and that the hair of the corpse in the photograph is too pale. There are two problems with this. First, even if Fairclough is right, another of Mary's nicknames was 'Fair Emma', which may imply that her hair was paler than Fairclough believes and second, the shades of grey in Victorian photographs are notoriously deceptive. The frogging on hussars' tunics, for example, appears in some portraits to be the same colour as the garments themselves (dark blue). In fact, in all cases it was bright yellow.

The other bombshell that Fairclough drops is the fate of Clarence. Far from dying, either of syphilis or flu in January 1892, he lived on to survive a murder attempt (again at the behest of Churchill) carried out by John Netley and Frederico Albericci, known as 'American Freddie' or 'Fingers Freddie', a small-time East End criminal who may have been employed by William Gull as a footman at his town house in Brook Street. Clarence was imprisoned in Glamis Castle, with its history of strange secrets and locked rooms. Here he lived, reading, painting, broken in spirit, until his death from natural causes in 1933.

Again, where do we start? The Sickert-Fairclough version relies on the monstrosity of Freemasonry, the declining mental state of Lord Randolph Churchill, the existence of an unproved clandestine marriage, the accuracy of the memory of Caroline Maxwell and the legitimacy of the Abberline diaries. Fascinating though the theory is, very little of it makes rational sense and none of it is 100 percent reliable.

0

STRIP JACK NAKED

We serial killers are your sons, we are your husbands, we are everywhere. And there will be more of your children dead tomorrow.

Ted Bundy

The Victorian police missed Jack the Ripper because they were looking for the wrong man. The science of criminology, such as it was in 1888, pointed to a dribbling lunatic with mad, staring eyes and glaring homicidal tendencies. Thus, when Dr William Holt, a houseman from St George's Hospital, leapt out on Mrs Humphreys in George Yard on November 11 1888, it was assumed that his spectacles and black-painted face were the clear hallmarks of a maniac. The papers took the nonsense further the next day, describing his glasses as white rings painted around his eyes. The 'white-eyed man' was roughed up by the crowd and had to be rescued by the police, to whom he explained he was looking for Jack in a variety of disguises. A similar oddball accosted Sarah Roney five days earlier in Brushfield Street, asking her to come along with him. She and her friend asked him what he carried in his black bag. 'Something the ladies don't like', he told them. And Sarah Lewis was terrified of a man in Bethnal Green Road on November 5 who had lured her down a passageway and began to open his coat to feel for something.

What we are dealing with here is terror. It is more than likely that Sarah Roney and Sarah Lewis were prostitutes and the men they describe just clients. Before Polly Nichols' murder, they wouldn't have given them a second thought, but accepted their tanner and hitched up their skirts ready for business. Around the time of Mary Kelly's death, any man was regarded with suspicion.

And if the run of the mill inhabitant of the Abyss and the copper on his beat had a preconceived idea of the fiend they were running from or looking for, educated men like Melville McNaghten were equally wide of the mark. Of M.J. Druitt, the Assistant Chief Constable wrote 'He was sexually insane.' Of Aaron Kosminski - 'this man became insane owing to many years indulgence in solitary vices'. And of Michael Ostrog, he was 'subsequently detained in a lunatic asylum as a homicidal maniac'. In all this, McNaghten is probably only describing the accepted psychiatric dogma of his day.

Two years after the Ripper struck, Henry Havelock Ellis went into print with *The Criminal* and lamented the fact that England had not kept in step with other countries in the field of criminal psychology - 'no book, scarcely a solitary magazine article, dealing with this matter, has appeared among us.' Ellis uses the term 'criminal anthropology' and divides this into physical and psychical components. Criminals, he says, are of certain types - 'political', 'by passion' and 'insane'. It is this last category that most obviously fits the Ripper, although nowhere in the book does Ellis mention him.

PLATE IV.

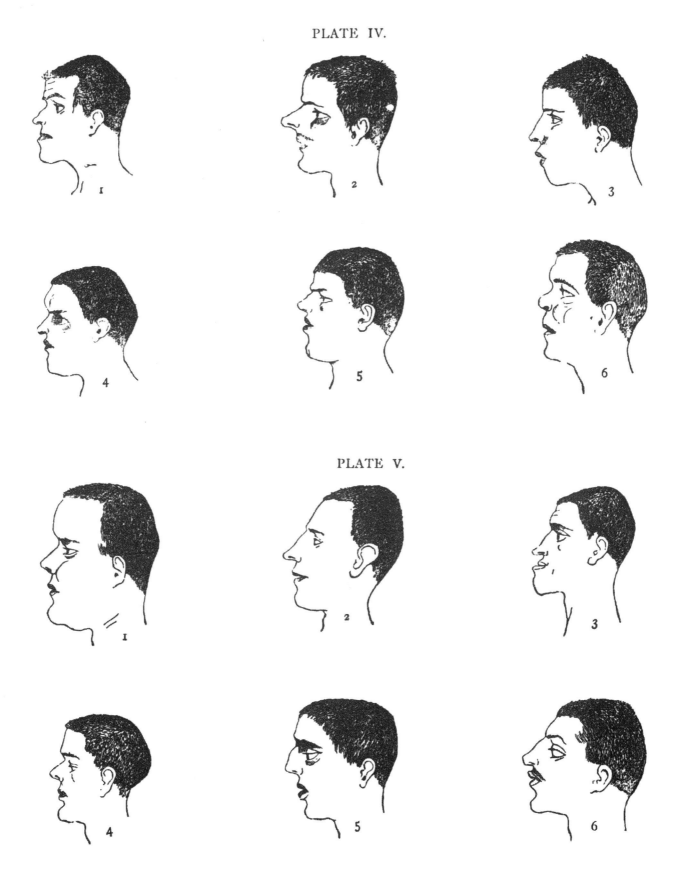

PLATE V.

Criminal 'types' from Havelock Ellis's 'The Criminal' (1907). All twelve are listed by initials, age, crime and background.
There are no murderers among them, because convicted murderers were usually hanged.

According to his figures, about 100 people a year were imprisoned in this country who were found to be insane - we have met several of them in this book. And ominously, Ellis acknowledges his - and everybody else's - lack of ability to cope with them:

> The lunatic may be influenced by the same motives that influence the sane person, but he is at the same time impelled by other motives peculiar to himself, and to which we may have no means of access.

He quotes European authorities such as Professor Enrico Ferri and Dr Napoleone Colajanni in their attempts to clarify motivation. The cosmic causes of crime include temperature and diet; the biological include anatomy, physiology, psychology; and the 'social factor' deals with 'the price of alcohol' and 'the price of wheat'. Ellis draws heavily on the work of Cesare Lombroso, the genius-of-all-trades whose 'L'Uomo Delinquente' ('Criminal Man') was then so influential in the medico-legal world. 'Sycopathia [sic] Sexualis' (in Chief Inspector Littlechild's letter to journalist G.R. Sims), the book by Krafft-Ebbing, scarcely rates a mention in Ellis.

It didn't help Littlechild and other earnest policemen trying to find their way through the fog of ignorance that in Britain there was not only no recent publication, but no organization where such things were discussed. And when the International Association of Criminal Law was set up by Dutch, German and Belgian authorities the year after the Ripper struck, England was less well represented than Serbia and Argentina!

Although he concedes that physical characteristics are less valuable as pointers to criminal types than they were, Ellis is still of the opinion that the shape of the brain, the face, the ears and so on are useful in catching criminals. He produces six pages of profile drawings, little more than bad caricatures, of criminal types and notes, as a man impressed:

> the largest ear Frigerio [an Italian expert] has ever seen . . . was in a woman convicted of complicity in the murder of her husband.

The sexual offender, Ottolenghi noted (and this should have been helpful in apprehending Jack):

presents the most rectilinear nose, though he shows the undulating profile of nose more frequently than any other group of criminals.

Marro believed that sexual offenders were usually full-bearded, whereas the insane were often bald. In Italy at least (where Marro's careful measurements were made), most rapists were fair haired and blue eyed. Ellis's work on 129 'wanted' criminals on Scotland Yard files in 1889-90 was inconclusive on this point.

   The problem was that the experts of the 1880s did not have the guts to throw out the claptrap of earlier generations and start afresh. Seventy years earlier, the Parisian thief and thief-taker Vidocq had said:

> I do not need to see the whole of a criminal's face to recognize him as such; it is enough for me to catch his eye.

Professor Sergi witnessed such a killer, aged fifteen, in prison for butchering a cow with a billhook:

> Reserved, taciturn . . . now that he is in prison he has the appearance of a wild beast, the glance of a tiger.

Andrei Chikatilo, who was charged with fifty-three murders at his trial in 1991, put on such a display behind the steel bars of the dock. With his shaven head, wild eyes and snarl, he was exactly what contemporaries looked for in Jack the Ripper. In fact, Chikatilo was a mild, inoffensive-looking man in drab coat and horn-rimmed glasses, able to secure the trust of teenage boys and girls even at the height of the 'Russian Ripper' scare.

   Back in the Autumn of Terror, Lombroso's typical sexual offender had bright eyes; a cracked, rough voice; swollen lips and eyelids. Even more useful for the police, he was occasionally 'humpbacked or otherwise deformed':

> The eye of the habitual homicide is glassy, cold and fixed; his nose is often aquiline, beaked, reminding one of a bird of prey . . . the jaws are strong; the ears long; the cheek-bones large; the hair dark, curling, abundant; the beard often thin; the canine teeth much developed; the lips thin . . .

Had Jack ever been caught - and dissected - experts of Ellis's day would have expected to have found the following. He would probably have long arms, a weakness of the chest, heart disease and some genital peculiarity. Heredity would also have been a factor. Jack would probably have had an elderly father in what Dr Langdon Down called 'the period of decadence'. The tendency too was for criminal parents to produce criminal or degenerate children. An unbelievable family cited by Rossi quotes the father as being a violent alcoholic, convicted of fraud. Of the children, one son was 'a monster'; another born with webbed fingers; another a highway robber; another committed on a charge of wounding; while one sister was insane and the other a prostitute. Jack's eyesight would have been good and he was not likely to have been colour-blind. He might or might not be among the 20 percent of murderers who blushed. He would probably have been a smoker and he may have been more than usually sensitive to changing weather conditions.

It is unlikely that Jack would have shown remorse for his crimes. 'Moral insensibility' marked most of the murderers that Dostoevsky knew in Siberia. Bruce Thompson knew remorse from only three of 400 killers. The French authority Despine noted the case of an Albanian who killed a traveller and complained when caught that the cost of his bullets was more than the victim had on him! And the murderer Thomas Wainewright, when asked how he could murder such an innocent girl as Helen Abercrombie, said 'Upon my soul, I don't know, unless it was because she had such thick legs.'

As far as intelligence goes, Jack was likely to have been fairly stupid, but this was more than compensated for by animal cunning. He would have been vain, an egotist. As Vidocq noted - 'to be an assassin is the highest praise'. And Ellis quotes an anonymous murderer - 'I want to do something great: oh, I shall be talked about!' He may have been sentimental, fond of animals; and Inspector Byrne, the New York policemen involved in the search for Tumblety, reminded his readers that 'nearly all the great criminals . . . are men who lead double lives.' Jack may well have been devout, or at least gone through the motions. A Mr Kennan, quoted by Ellis, wrote:

> A Russian peasant may be . . . a murderer, but he continues nevertheless to cross himself and say his prayers.

So might an inhabitant of the Abyss.

Dr Laurent, an expert on prisoners, wrote of their wall-scribblings, but he might have been writing about Jack:

sex is not for them a sacred and mysterious thing, a mystic rose hidden beneath the obscure vault of the body, like a strange and precious talisman enclosed in a tabernacle. For them it is a thing of ugliness, which they drag into the light of day and laugh at.

Robert Anderson, Assistant Commissioner at the Yard, tried to get a handle on the man who was Jack the Ripper:

> One did not need to be Sherlock Holmes to discover that the criminal was a sexual maniac of a virulent type; that he was living in the immediate vicinity of the scenes of the murders; and that, if he was not living absolutely alone, his people knew of his guilt.

Modern criminologists would agree that here Anderson is probably right on the button, but then he veered off to accuse the 'low class' Jews because he thought he knew who the Ripper was.

Dr Thomas Bond, who carried out the post-mortems on Mary Kelly, went further. Although the authors of *The Ripper A-Z* find that the doctor's deductions are of limited value, his last two points are a fascinating insight into the psychology of the day.

> The murderer [wrote Bond] must have been a man of physical strength and of great coolness and daring. There is no evidence that he had an accomplice. He must in my opinion be a man subject to periodical attacks of homicidal and erotic mania. The character of the mutilations indicate that the man may be in a condition sexually, that may be called satyriasis [the male version of nymphomania]. It is of course possible that the homicidal impulse may have developed from a revengeful or brooding condition of the mind, or that Religious Mania may have been the original disease, but I do not think either hypothesis is likely. The murderer in external appearance is quite likely to be a quiet, inoffensive looking man, probably middle-aged and neatly and respectably dressed. I think he must be in the habit of wearing a cloak or overcoat or he could hardly have escaped notice in the streets if blood on his hands or clothes were visible.

And Bond goes on:

> Assuming the murderer to be such a person as I have just described he would probably be solitary and eccentric in his habits, also he is most likely to be a man without regular occupation, but with some small income or pension. He is possibly living among respectable persons who have some knowledge of his character and habits and who may have grounds for suspicion that he is not quite right in his mind at times.

We have moved on. Jack the Ripper is regarded now as the first example in history of the serial killer, and Richard von Krafft-Ebbing outlined the M.O. which the medico-legal world still recognizes:

> It is probable that he first cut the throats of his victims, then ripped open the abdomen and groped among the intestines. In some instances he cut off the genitals and carried them away; in others he only tore them to pieces and left them behind. He does not seem to have had sexual intercourse with his victims, but very likely the murderous act and subsequent mutilation of the corpse were the equivalent of the sex act.

There is a problem with the definition of a serial killer, but most experts agree that we are talking about someone who kills at least three unrelated victims with a space between each - an 'emotional cooling off period' (as Schecter and Everitt describe it in the *A-Z Encyclopedia of Serial Killers*) which can last from hours to years. It is this last fact which has eluded most Ripper researchers and has led them to look in the wrong direction for Jack. Most experts agree too that the true serial killer is a sadist, so that widows and even nurses who murder quietly for financial gain do not fall into this category.

There are no killers in British history who fit this bill before Jack. In Europe there are tall tales of Gilles de Rais, the Marshal of France who was a black magician and child-eater; and Elizabeth Bathory, the Transylvanian werewolf-princess who had hundreds of young girls slaughtered so that she could restore her beauty by bathing in blood. These should be taken with a pinch of salt, simply because powerful people like de Rais and Bathory had malicious enemies and because the evidence simply isn't there.

Why then did the autumn of 1888 give rise to the world's first serial killer? Karl Marx's view is alienation. By the late 19th century, the world - especially the world of industrial Britain - had become machine-centred. Earlier writers, like the pamphleteering radical William Cobbett and the Chartist Feargus O'Connor had warned of the evils of industrialization. Cobbett, from his 'little village' of Kensington could see London, 'the great wen', visibly encroaching across the fields. O'Connor wanted to take mill workers out of their hellish rut and re-install them in rural hamlets. But you can't stop 'progress'. By 1888, London was the biggest city in the world, not yet eclipsed by New York and Chicago. People became lost in this terrifying new world of steam and noise and the pursuit of money. Those who could, coped; those who couldn't, went to the wall. Or more accurately, to the bottom of Jack London's Abyss. It is there we will find Jack the Ripper - lost in an alien world with which he could not cope. His answer was to lash out and for personal reasons we cannot know, because we do not know who he was, the conscious targets of his unconscious bewilderment were five sad women who had never done him any harm.

How close can we get to this man? Are we able to strip him naked in the full glare of modern psychiatric methods? The first attempt at 'profiling' was carried out by Dr James Brussel of New York in the 1950s who predicted with astonishing accuracy the probable lifestyle of a maniac who was planting explosive devices all over the city. Brussel believed his 'mad bomber' would be a middle-aged man, of Eastern European origin, living with a female relative and suffering from a series of physical illnesses. He would be polite, a churchgoer and would wear a double-breasted suit. While all this sounds like one of the more ludicrous passages from Conan Doyle, where Sherlock Holmes and his gigantic brain are in action, it transpired that Brussel was right. The bomber was George Metesky, a fifty-four year old Pole who lived with his sisters, never missed church on Sundays and had been treated for tuberculosis.

What emerged from all this was the Federal Bureau of Investigation's Behavioural Science Unit and in particular the Criminal Personality Profiling Program. Over twenty years of careful study of notorious American serial killers - men like Ted Bundy, John Wayne Gacy, Dean Korll - have enabled psychiatrists to plumb the warped minds of individuals who in previous generations would never have been caught (like Jack), or would have been executed without any questions being asked.

Whereas we have established a Victorian profile of Jack from Henry Havelock Ellis's writings, a modern one looks like this. He would probably have been a bed-wetter (over 60 percent of serial killers were still soaking their sheets in their teens). He may have been fascinated with fires, experimenting with arson and delighting in the flare and roar of the flames. One wonders if, along with half the East End, Jack was watching the fire in the docks an hour or so before he killed Polly Nichols in Bucks Row. He would have had sadistic urges from the age of seven or eight, ripping the wings off flies or torturing cats. This is the famous 'triad', the three danger signs in young children, although of course not all exhibitioners of all three tendencies go on to become serial killers.

The types of serial killers - the motivation for their crimes - have a tendency to overlap. There is little doubt that Jack was a psychopath, that is he had no conscience or sense of wrong-doing, but beyond that common assertion, he fits the mission-oriented killer. Although the phrase 'I am down on whores' was written by a hoaxer, there is little doubt that Jack was of the same view. All five of his victims were prostitutes and we hear echoes of Peter Sutcliffe, the Yorkshire Ripper, who saw himself as 'the street cleaner':

> The women I killed were filth - bastard prostitutes who were littering the streets. I was just cleaning up the place a bit.

Sutcliffe had chosen to ignore the fact that several of his victims were not prostitutes at all. It is this sort of thinking that created the idea of the deranged social worker - Thomas Barnardo or Frederick Charrington, as some would have it - determined to reform society by any means at their disposal.

It is also possible that Jack was a hedonistic killer. To men like this, murder and mutilation are ends in themselves - 'just for jolly'. Such killers obtain relief, sometimes sexual, sometimes not, from their work. When the Russian Ripper, Andrei Chikatilo, was finally caught after years of effort by the police, he said 'What I did was not for sexual pleasure. Rather it brought me some peace of mind.'

Lastly, Jack may have been a power-seeker. Most psychiatrists today believe that violent sex crimes, such as rape and murder, have less to do with sex than with the will to dominate. When Polly Nichols, Annie Chapman, Liz Stride, Kate Eddowes and Mary

Kelly went down before his knife, Jack controlled them. They were his playthings, like dolls, that he could break at will.

In 1984, Special Agent Robert K. Ressler of the FBI presented a paper to the International Association of Forensic Sciences, listing the characteristics of serial killers. Its usefulness in the case of Jack is limited, because the FBI are using American 20th century criminals as their raw material and as a historian, I believe these to be a world away from the dregs of humanity that Lombroso and Ellis described a century ago. Over 90 percent of Ressler's killers were white males (so was Jack, but in the Abyss of 1888 it would be unlikely he'd be anything else). They were intelligent with IQs at the 'bright normal' level (this is in sharp contrast to Ellis's view on the stupidity of criminals). They worked at jobs which did not fulfil them, having seriously underachieved at school. We have no way of knowing whether Jack attended school or not. Compulsory education was not established by law until Sandon's Act of 1876 and was not a reality for many years to come. Ressler's killers came from unstable families, often abandoned by their fathers and dominated by their mothers (in the Abyss, such families were everywhere). They often had criminal and alcoholic histories (so did many families in the Abyss). They hated their parents and were often physically and sexually abused as children (sexual abuse was a taboo subject in Victorian England, so very little evidence for it exists. Physical abuse, however, abounded). They often had a record of psychiatric problems as children (given the lack of facilities, care and medical knowledge in the 1870s - when Jack was a boy - it is most unlikely that any of this would be noticed and it certainly wouldn't be dealt with). Most of Ressler's killers were interested in voyeurism and vicious pornography from an early age (the latter was available in the 1870s, but in limited quantities because of its cost, much of it being imported from France. The former was no problem. The chronic overcrowding of the Abyss and the couples having sex in courts and alleyways created a paradise for the pervert).

In the centenary of the Ripper murders, 1988, the FBI were asked to provide a profile specifically for Jack. They came to the conclusion that he was a male in his late twenties, who lived in the area and was not hamstrung by family commitments. He had no surgical skill and was a loner, possibly with a police conviction. It is likely that he was abused as a child, probably by his mother. Is that as close as we can get?

Dr Joel Norris is probably the world's leading expert on serial sexual murder and he has identified seven phases by which the killer operates. Do they fit Jack's nocturnal wanderings? We cannot guess at the aura phase, that first time that Jack began to withdraw into his own private world of perverted fantasy. The fantasies became more real, the urge more insistent until he was compelled, on Friday August 31, to act. Next comes the trawling phase, Jack prowling the Abyss in search of a victim. Did he see Polly Nichols talking to Ellen Holland at the corner of Brick Lane and Osborn Street? Is that when he pounced? Again, in the early hours of Saturday September 8, did he trail 'Dark Annie' along Hanbury Street, watching her, making sure she was alone? And on Saturday September 29, at what time did he notice 'Long Liz' Stride meandering along Berner Street in search of trade? Frustrated and furious at the interruption in Dutfield's Yard, did he then 'trawl' west and see his next victim, Kate Eddowes, standing a little tipsily near Church Passage that led to Mitre Square? And finally, on the morning of November 9, did he catch sight of 'Ginger' or 'Fair Emma' wandering in Dorset Street, perhaps still singing snatches of 'Only a violet I plucked from my mother's grave'?

The wooing phase is rather a misnomer for Jack's behaviour. Joel Norris is thinking of smooth charmers like Ted Bundy, who feigned injury to lure girls into his car or John Wayne Gacy who offered young men jobs. The timescale of the Ripper killings precluded much of that, although those who saw Jack with his victims remembered calm, friendly conversation. Outside Number 29 Hanbury Street, just before he led her along the dark passageway to her death, he asked Annie Chapman 'Will you?' She signed her death warrant by saying 'Yes'. If it *was* Jack seen with Liz Stride near Number 64 Berner Street, the couple were joking together - 'You would say anything but your prayers.' And if this was Jack, it's an important piece of evidence because of the obvious intimacy of the phrase. Either Jack knew Liz or he was able to strike up disarmingly friendly conversations quickly. And George Hutchinson heard Mary Kelly say to Jack, 'Alright, my dear. Come along, you will be comfortable.'

The capture phase comes next. This was the moment when Jack struck, suddenly, powerfully, perhaps from behind in the first instance, at least for his first four victims. He grabbed their throats with iron fingers, strangling them into unconsciousness. Then, the murder itself - the slashing knife across the throat, the mutilations on the ground. This is the pinnacle of pleasure. This is what the weeks or months of waiting have been leading to.

Then the totem phase. Jack, in common with all serial killers, would want to prolong the experience of killing, to carry out an action replay of the crime. So he took a trophy from his victims - perhaps the rings (though it seems unlikely) from Annie Chapman, the kidney and uterus from Kate Eddowes, along with half her apron and, most telling of all, he stole the heart from Mary Kelly.

The final phase is the depression phase. All emotions spent, the murderer can become suicidal, but more often he merely builds up yet another craving for blood and the seven-phase cycle begins again. In the annals of American crime since 1945 not a single known serial killer has committed suicide. In Britain, only one has - the multiple murderer Fred West.

How much of this psychological analysis, ancient and modern, can we go along with? Jack the Ripper lived locally, in either Whitechapel or Spitalfields. No one who didn't know the area like the back of his hand could use those courts and alleys in the way Jack did. He was not a Jew. There is nothing in the behaviour of the immigrants of the 1880s to suggest violence of this type. That leaves us with the locals - Jack was an Irish Cockney. And he was employed - which is why he struck at weekends, because his job kept him too pinned down in the week. He was in his late twenties or early thirties and had enough income to be able to vary his clothes. They were not disguises in the accepted sense, but gave sufficient variety so that the same description never quite appears twice in police records or newspaper articles. He was probably single and lived on his own and for that reason alone was probably interviewed by the police, perhaps on more than one occasion. The Yorkshire police interviewed Peter Sutcliffe nine times before they caught him. Jack had surgical skill of a limited type. He was probably a slaughterman or Billingsgate fishmarket porter and he did not commit suicide, neither was he incarcerated in a lunatic asylum.

It is in the depression phase that Jack escaped. This phase can last for hours, weeks, months or years. So rather than combing asylums for patients admitted within months of the event or scouring the obituaries for deaths, suicidal or accidental before 1890, we ought to widen the net considerably - and the wider it becomes, the colder the trail gets.

I personally believe we will never know the identity of Jack the Ripper. I hope I am wrong. I hope that somehow, diligent research, a lucky break, *something* will give us the information we lack at the moment. And, if that day comes, I will stand up with all the historians, criminologists and Ripperologists in the world and say -

'Who?'

Polly Nichols died in Bucks Row to the right of centre of this map, north of the Whitechapel Road.

Annie Chapman's body was found in Hanbury Street in the centre of this map.

The body of Liz Stride was discovered in Dutfield's yard off Berner Street in the centre of this map.

The second victim of the double event, Kate Eddowes, was found in Mitre Square, near Duke Street in the centre of this map.

The last of the Ripper's victims, Mary Kelly, was found in Miller's Court off Dorset Street in the centre of this map.

Bibliography and Index

Murder and Madness: The Secret Life of Jack the Ripper
David Abrahamsen 1992

The True Face of Jack the Ripper
Melvyn Harris 1994

The Jack the Ripper A-Z
Paul Begg, Martin Fido, Keith Skinner 1996

Autumn of Terror
Tom Cullen 1965

The Rise of Scotland Yard
Douglas Browne 1956

Jack the Ripper: the Mystery Solved
Paul Harrison 1991

Jack the Ripper in Fact and Fiction
Robin Odell 1966

Jack the Ripper
Daniel Farson 1972

The Complete Jack the Ripper
Donald Rumbelow 1988

Jack the Ripper: the Final Solution
Stephen Knight 1984

Will the Real Jack the Ripper?
Arthur Douglas 1979

The Crimes, Detection and Death of Jack the Ripper
Martin Fido 1987

Jack the Ripper: the Bloody Truth
Melvyn Harris 1987

Jack the Ripper: 100 Years of Investigation
Terence Sharkey 1987

The Ripper and the Royals
Melvyn Fairclough 1992

The Diary of Jack the Ripper
Shirley Harrison 1993

The Complete History of Jack the Ripper
Philip Sugden 1995

Jack the Ripper: First American Serial Killer
Stuart Evans and Paul Gainey 1995

Jack the Ripper: The Simple Truth
Bruce Paley 1995

The A-Z of Serial Killers
Harold Schechter and David Everitt 1996

Living London
George Sims 1903

Madame Tussaud's Chamber of Horrors
Pauline Chapman 1986

Jack the Ripper: Summing Up and Verdict
Colin Wilson and Robin Odell 1988

A Century of Sex Killers
Brian Marriner 1992

The Criminal Hand
Patricia Marne 1991

Serial Killers
Joel Norris 1990

Oscar Wilde's London
Eckhardt, Gilman & Chamberlain 1987

40 Years of Scotland Yard
F. Wensley 1931

Infamous Murders
1975

Punch: or the London Charivari
1888

The Criminal
H. Havelock Ellis 1891

The Streets of East London
William Fishman 1992

1888
William Fishman 1988

The People of the Abyss
Jack London 1903

Murder Guide to London
Martin Fido 1986

The Murders of the Black Museum
Gordon Honeycombe 1984

Criminals and Crime
Robert Anderson 1907

The Scotland Yard Files
Paul Begg and Keith Skinner 1992

The Fifty Most Amazing Crimes of the Last 100 Years
ed. Parrish and Crosland 1936

Hangmen of England
Brian Bailey 1989

Hunting the Devil
Richard Lourie 1993

The Mammoth Book of True Crime
Colin Wilson 1988

The Murderers' Who's Who
Gauté and Odell 1980

Murder: 'Whatdunnit'
Gauté and Odell 1982

Index

Index

Index